Lemuel Abijah Abbott

Personal Recollections and Civil War Diary, 1864

© 2025, Lemuel Abijah Abbott (domaine public)
Édition : BoD · Books on Demand, 31 avenue Saint-Rémy, 57600 Forbach, bod@bod.fr
Impression : Libri Plureos GmbH, Friedensallee 273, 22763 Hamburg (Allemagne)
ISBN : 978-2-3226-1390-8
Dépôt légal : Avril 2025

been very cold all day. This afternoon I have been papering my hut so our quarters are quite comfortable now. The band has been out this evening and played some very pretty pieces, and I am thankful for it relieves the monotony of dull camp life. This evening Lieut. D. G. Hill and Captain Goodrich, the brigade Quartermaster, called; they were in fine spirits. It is bitter cold, but no wind as last night; have received no letters which of course is provoking.

SUNDAY, Jan. 3, 1864.

Quite a comfortable day; no snow yet, but it looks likely to storm in a day or two; wrote to Pert, and had our usual inspection this forenoon. Since dinner, I have read "Washington's Farewell Address", and the "Declaration of Independence". This evening quite a number of recruits arrived for the regiment, but none for Company B. Capt. J. A. Salisbury has been in to call on Lieut. Stetson, and broken my camp chair. This is still more provoking than not to get a letter from home for chairs are not plentiful here. He is a big man.

MONDAY, Jan. 4, 1864.

It has snowed nearly all day, but not very hard. To-night there is about two inches on the ground and it is still snowing. Lieut. Stetson started for Vermont this morning on the 9:30 train, and Capt. H. R. Steele arrived from there this evening. I am told to-night that Colonel Embic of the One Hundred and Sixth New York Infantry has been reinstated. We have formed a quiz school to-night, the members being Dr. Almon Clark, Lieuts. E. P. Farr and C. G. Newton and Chaplain E. M. Haynes. We are to meet every night and ask questions on geography, history, etc. I think it a grand idea. I suspect they think me fresh from school, though, and want me to do most of the quizzing, the same as in the class of about seventy-five enlisted men in tactics and English branches which recites to me daily now, fitting for examination for commission in colored troops.

TUESDAY, Jan. 5. 1864.

It has been a beautiful day, but the wind is blowing very chilly to-night; drew clothing for the Company this afternoon; had a very good dress parade considering the quantity of snow and mud under foot. Our school met this evening but we didn't accomplish much. Capt. E. B. Frost, and Dr. W. A. Child and wife dined with us to-day; had a nice time. Herbert George, the band master, has been in this evening relating his experiences during his leave in Vermont. It almost makes me homesick: have got to go on picket early in the morning beyond Culpeper, Va.

WEDNESDAY, Jan. 6, 1864.

Chilly and cloudy but the weather is moderating very fast; got cheated out of my breakfast this morning on account of going on picket; formed line at 7.45 and so remained till nearly 10 a. m. when the officer of the day came and started us for the picket line; got on the wrong road and did not find the line until 3 p. m. It has been quite pleasant all day, but looks likely to storm before morning. No mail to-day.

THURSDAY, Jan. 7, 1864.

Quite cold and disagreeable; got up about 10 a. m. feeling as well as could be expected after a hard day's march. The men had been to breakfast and were in fine spirits; were relating their experiences in the late engagement at Locust Grove. Banty—a little, jolly, duck-legged Frenchman—started for camp this forenoon for more rations and the mail, but after he had been gone about a half hour a man from Company E. came from camp with both. The weather has moderated and it is snowing this evening.

FRIDAY, Jan. 8. 1864.

It cleared during the night and this morning it was sharp and cold. As I awoke the sun was peeping brilliantly up behind the eastern hills and all nature was beautiful. About two inches of snow fell in the night which added to the beauty of the sunrise. Three deserters stole into our lines from the enemy in the night. They report that many more want to get away; read two letters to-night one from home and one from Hen.

SATURDAY, Jan. 9, 1864.

Still the weather continues fine. There is not a cloud to be seen or a breath of air stirring, and yet it is quite a sharp morning. The Company got another mail this forenoon but there was nothing for me; was relieved from picket this afternoon about one o'clock: arrived in camp about four p. m.; found plenty of Company work to keep me busy all tomorrow. Lieut. C. G. Newton started for Vermont this morning; have been studying tactics this evening; got my books from home I sent for last week.

SUNDAY, Jan. 10, 1864.

A beautiful morning. Dan Bancroft came in to see me this forenoon, a private in the Vermont Cavalry; had inspection at 11 a. m. and dress parade this evening. Quite a number of recruits came this evening, but only one for Company B. Col. A. B. Jewett and Lieut.-Colonel W. W. Henry also returned from Vermont to-night. The band has been serenading Colonel Jewett. It is cold and frosty with a little snow still on the ground.

MONDAY, Jan. 11, 1864.

Another fine day; have been very busy attending to Company matters; also received many calls—in fact it has taken me a goodly part of the day to entertain visitors. Capt. Samuel Darrah, Herbert George of the band and Lieut. W. R. Hoyt have just gone and now comes Lieut. E. P. Farr, and it's after 10 o'clock; haven't studied a bit to-day, yet, but I shall make up for lost time before I sleep.

Tuesday, Jan. 12, 1864.

Retired at 2 a. m. last night; learned by heart before retiring fifty pages in tactics; got up at 9 a. m. and went at it again; have conquered fifty pages more to-day and recited them to Lieut. Farr: had them fairly well learned before; only review; weather warm and comfortable; had a dress parade at 5 p. m. This evening twenty recruits armed and equipped arrived from Vermont for Company B; got some newspapers from cousin Abby Burnham to-night.

Wednesday, Jan. 13, 1864.

It has been very muddy and dull in camp to-day; weather dark and gloomy: no dress parade; have written to Pert; also received a letter from J. R. Seaver, containing a plan of the hospitals being built at Montpelier, now nearly completed. Lieut. Farr has been in this evening and we have been studying tactics together; guess he takes advantage of my being better posted than he, having been a cadet at Norwich University, Norwich, Vermont, where I was well drilled, and can explain things better. I wish they didn't consider me the best drill in the regiment; it makes me lots of extra work and takes much time. But I must be obliging—not mean and selfish.

Thursday, Jan. 14, 1864.

The weather still continues to be warm and pleasant; no wind and not a cloud in sight; have received two letters from Vermont to-night—one from home and another from one of my old scholars in Chelsea. The teachers who succeeded me in my school there had very poor success both last summer and this winter. When the teacher announced to the school this winter one morning that I had died of typhoid fever at Rockville, Md., it having been so reported, the children refused to be reconciled and grieved so they had to be dismissed, the same thing occurring the next morning. Poor things! I never think of it but what my eyes—well, my throat gets lumpy and my lips quiver. I had no idea they were so devoted. It seems as though they would follow me in memory throughout eternity. Still, as their teacher I was strict and firm, but always just, and never struck one of the flock of sixty during either winter with them. Will I ever make such devoted friends again? Alas! it's only a memory now but will ever be a sacred one. May the recollection be as blissful to them as it will be to me throughout the everlasting ages of time. Nothing has occurred to-day worthy of note; have had my cabin full all day. Lieuts. W. R. Hoyt and E. P.

Farr have been in this evening.

FRIDAY, Jan. 15, 1864.

It is by far the finest day we have had this year, but very muddy. A part of the regiment has gone on picket to remain three days. It is reported in camp that one entire regiment of "Johnnies" came over from Cedar Mountain this morning and gave itself up. They were miserably clad, a large majority having no shoes at all; they started for Washington this evening. It's a beautiful moonlight night.

SATURDAY, Jan. 16, 1864.

Another warm summer day; have been at work on clothing rolls, also laying down sidewalk in front of my quarters. One of our new recruits has gone to the hospital to-day sick with lung fever. General W. H. Morris has returned from his home near N. Y. city with his sister and a lady friend. This evening he rode through the camp and was cheered by the men. The bands are serenading him to-night, his headquarters being just about a hundred yards in rear of my hut. It is bright moonlight.

SUNDAY, Jan. 17, 1864.

It has been a cold and disagreeable day; had Company inspection this forenoon; have written home to-night; received a letter from Carl Wilson and one from Pert; wind blew hard this forenoon, but it is calm to-night; band played this evening. Five more recruits arrived this afternoon for Company B. It's cloudy and looks like rain.

MONDAY, Jan. 18, 1864.

It has rained hard all day, but is not very cold. The mud is very deep. It's rumored that Governor Smith and Mr. Baxter are to be here to-morrow; have been studying hard all day only when engaged in Company duty; cooler this evening; snows a little; pickets have just come in wet and tired. Lieut. E. P. Farr has not been in this evening to look up tactics.

TUESDAY, Jan. 19, 1864.

The wind has been blowing furiously all day from the northwest; has rained very little; commencing to freeze this evening; have been looking over ordnance returns this afternoon; no time to study to-day. Lieut. Ezra Stetson is expected to-morrow, also Governor Smith, as he didn't come to-night. Lieut. D. G. Hill has been in this evening; wind blows a gale.

WEDNESDAY, Jan. 20, 1864.

Quite a fine moon to-night—a little cloudy but no wind; froze quite hard last night; have had so much company all day it has been impossible to do anything but visit; band is serenading General W. H. Morris; are proud of our band, it being one of best regimental bands in the army. Lieut. Stetson has not come tonight; got no letter from home, but received a good one from Carl Wilson. To-night they have the Universalist festival at Barre, Vt.; would like to be there, but my festival will be with tactics.

THURSDAY, Jan. 21, 1864.

It was quite frosty this morning, but pleasant and has remained so all day; had regimental monthly inspection this forenoon. Company B got the credit of having the best street in the brigade. I am proud of my old Company; it always tries to please me. Nate Harrington and Orry Blanchard of the First Vermont Brigade have been to see me to-day. Lieut. Ezra Stetson has not come to-night, his time being up last Tuesday; no letter from home yet; beautiful moonlight night, but quite cool.

FRIDAY, Jan. 22, 1864.

As pleasant a morning as I ever saw. Lieut. D. G. Hill started for Vermont this forenoon; have made out the final statements of Corporals C. W. Beal, C. B. Lee and Private A. S. Parkhurst, but Lee is dangerously ill in the hospital and not able to receive his discharge papers. Private J. W. Sawyer, a recruit in B Company has been in hospital but is gaining fast; received a letter from home this evening. Lieut. Ezra Stetson has not come yet; fear he will find trouble when he does come.

SATURDAY, Jan. 23, 1864.

It has been a beautiful day with a light southern breeze; have not had a moment's time to myself all day someone being here all the time. It's provoking for I want to study so much. Beal and Parkhurst started for home to-day, Barre, Vt. Lieut. Ezra Stetson has not come yet. Major C. G. Chandler received a letter from Capt. E. Dillingham to-night, who is a prisoner of war at Richmond, Va. Private George G. Brown was detailed this evening in the Company mess house.

SUNDAY, Jan. 24, 1864.

The day has been fair; started for picket at 9 a.m.; relieved the One Hundred and Sixth New York Infantry about noon; made my headquarters at Mr. Bowen's, an old man about seventy-five years old; has a son who lives with him, a miller, which accounts for his not being drafted into the Confederate army. A "yaller girl", as we call them, keeps house for him. All's quiet on the picket line. It's a lovely night.

Monday, Jan. 25, 1864.

Still another fine night; have been reading the newspaper to the old gentleman, etc. Ain't I a good Yankee? One Johnny, a deserter, came into our lines last night; reports that an entire brigade of the enemy whose time has expired is fighting its way into our lines. Perhaps this may be true but I can't vouch for it. I take it with a grain of salt. It is evident, though, that a great number are deserting to our lines; have finished my Company clerk book to-day. The moon is shining brightly.

Tuesday, Jan. 26, 1864.

It has been a lovely day. Some of the time it's been really uncomfortable, the sun has been so warm. About 1 a. m. last night when making the rounds considerable firing was heard towards the right of the line. It was probably deserters trying to come into our lines. Sergeant Daniel Foster came to the picket line this afternoon to get some money to send Corporal C. B. Lee's remains to Vermont who died last evening. Banty has come with some rations. Lieut. Ezra Stetson arrived in camp Sunday evening.

Wednesday, Jan. 27, 1864.

It has been a delightful day; expect to be relieved this afternoon. Two deserters came into our lines this morning; they report Lee's army in a miserable condition—no rations or clothing, and the citizens nearly starving. They say that "Secession is playing out." The Thirty-eighth Pennsylvania Infantry relieved us about noon; arrived in camp about 5 p. m. The roads are in splendid condition, as good as I ever saw them in Virginia at this time of year. If the weather was fine all the time picket guard would be more desirable than so much camp duty.

Thursday, Jan. 28, 1864.

A fine morning. Most of the companies have been fixing their streets; have been at work all day on Lieut. Ezra Stetson's ordnance returns, and have not got them done yet; will try and finish them in the morning. The regiment got no mail to-night. Corporal C. B. Lee's remains were sent home Tuesday; had a dress parade to-night in which the recruits took part. Those of Company B never had a gun in their hands till this morning.

Friday, Jan. 29, 1864.

It has been really uncomfortable all day, it's been so warm. Lieut G. E. Davis started for Vermont this forenoon; have completed the ordnance return but it's not mailed yet. Most of the officers have been playing ball this afternoon. The non-commissioned officers have given us a challenge to play for the oysters to-morrow, and the Colonel has accepted it; received a letter from brother Roy and wife and one from home; have been reading army regulations, etc. Colonel A. B. Jewett has refused to approve Lieut. E. P. Farr's application.

SATURDAY, Jan. 30, 1864.

A cloudy, chilly day, but not much rain. One game of ball came off this afternoon in which the commissioned officers won. Two more games are to be played Monday if a good day. It's a cloudy, dark, gloomy evening in camp; haven't studied much to-day, but read army regulations some. Dr. W. A. Child and Lieuts. H. H. Dewey and E. P. Farr have been in this evening.

SUNDAY, Jan. 31, 1864.

The wind has been whistling around the cabin all day. It's been misty, but we've had little rain; have been to church and written home. We have a goodly sized log chapel covered with the fly of the new hospital tent. Mrs. W. A. Child was present and sang, a rich treat, for it has been a long time since I've heard a lady's voice at church. Sergeant J. M. Read has been in this evening.

MONDAY, Feb. 1, 1864.

A dull and miserable day, but no rain; have been studying very hard in the second volume of tactics. No one has been in this evening save Lieut. George P. Welch who has notified me I am detailed for picket to-morrow. It is not my turn and is a great disappointment as I have laid my plans to accomplish a good week's work, and had this not happened, I could have sent in my application next week to appear before General Silas Casey's board in Washington for examination for a commission in colored troops. I want to be a field officer and won't accept anything else.

TUESDAY, Feb. 2, 1864.

A cloudy morning. The sick have gone to the general hospital to-day which indicates a general move; started for picket at 9 a. m.; fine marching; arrived on the line about 12 noon; heavy wind all afternoon; am in command of Company G on picket; have had a thunderstorm this evening. All's quiet on the picket line to-night.

WEDNESDAY, Feb. 3, 1864.

High wind, cloudy but no rain all day; have moved my tent down by the men's, so am quite comfortable to-night. The officer of the day came along about 4 a. m.; all was quiet along the line during the night. The countersign is "Mexico." My rations are getting very short.

THURSDAY, Feb. 4, 1864.

A fine morning, Captain Samuel Darrah has been down; have sent to camp for the mail and more rations; quite a comfortable day. All's been quiet through the day, but to-night there's been some firing both sides of my post along the line; mail has come but no letter for me. The countersign is "Vera Cruz." It's a beautiful night.

Friday, Feb. 5, 1864.

It has been very much like a beautiful spring morning in Vermont. I wish that I were there to take a walk on the snow crust, but this at present cannot be; were relieved from picket about 1 p. m. by the One Hundred and Twenty-second Ohio Infantry. It is quite cloudy this evening and bids fair for a stormy day to-morrow; received a good letter from home this evening, and have reviewed part fourth in the second volume of tactics.

Saturday, Feb. 6, 1864.

I was awoke at 5 a. m. by the long roll; was soon directed to report to Col. A. B. Jewett's headquarters and ordered to break camp and march for the Rapidan, which is no pleasant thing to do at this season; were ordered to march at 7 a. m. but didn't till near 4 p. m.; marched to the picket line and bivouacked; has rained some all day but not hard; considerable firing towards night at Jacob's ford.

Sunday, Feb. 7, 1864.

Resumed our march at daylight; halted about two miles from the river and remained through the day. The Johnnies were on this very ground yesterday in large numbers, but were repulsed by the First Corps and fled across the river; no fighting to-day; got orders about sundown to return to camp which we did without a halt. On arrival there we found there had been a great scare from Mosby but it amounted to nothing; wonder if he thinks guerrilla warfare manly? Some people are born gorillas, though, and have no more conception of honor. I'd go and drown myself before I'd practice that kind of warfare!

Monday, Feb. 8, 1864.

Chilly and cloudy; don't feel very well to-day, nor does anyone else; all stiff and lame; don't wonder at it for we had to march through mud and water ankle deep or more last night from the Rapidan without a rest. The regiments were completely disorganized; officers and men all got lost from their commands and both struggled and straggled into camp as best they could. It was a mob and a disgrace to the Third Corps.

Tuesday, Feb. 9, 1864.

A chilly south wind has been blowing all day, and it looks likely to snow before night; hope it will for if it does not, I fear we will have to make another

Rapidan campaign which I am not at all anxious for. I have been over to Lieutenant Thompson's quarters studying to-day, as I have been so annoyed in my own quarters that I could not possibly study; am with Lieut. Ezra Stetson; got a paper from Pert to-night and a New Year's Address.

WEDNESDAY, Feb. 10, 1864.

The weather has been fine but rather cold with a chilly northeast wind; had a good brigade drill this afternoon. Col. A. B. Jewett had an officers' school this evening in the chapel which is very essential to us all. Lieut. Ezra. Stetson has commenced to build an addition to our hut, as he is expecting to have his wife come out and remain with him the rest of the winter.

THURSDAY, Feb. 11, 1864.

The weather has been clear and pleasant, but intensely cold for this latitude. Lieutenant C. F. Nye returned from Vermont this evening looking as rotund and hearty as ever; received a letter from home; all well; have got to start for a three-days' tour of picket to-morrow. Capt. H. R. Steele is officer of the day; wind blowing furiously to-night.

FRIDAY, Feb. 12, 1864.

Clear and cold but no wind; started for picket at 9 a. m.; arrived on the line at 1 p. m. A part of our detail having through mistake to go to Pony Mountain, has returned this evening, and consequently I have had to move my headquarters up the line; am near Mrs. Battles, historic because of Union officers' escapades there. The house being between the lines the women connived in trying to get them captured; countersign is "Perth."

SATURDAY, Feb. 13, 1864.

Clear and warm with no wind, and by far the finest day of the month yet. Captain H. R. Steele came along this morning and took a part of Companies B and G for the reserve thus leaving me in charge of only five posts; wonder what he's afraid of? Have received our mail, but none for me. All's quiet on the line to-night; countersign "Bristeau."

SUNDAY, Feb. 14, 1864.

Clear and chilly but very little wind; fields and woods in front of the line to-day all on fire. A squadron of Cavalry has been out on a scout to-day and captured Billy Scott and two or three of his comrades. He is a noted guerilla. It is also reported that our cavalry ran onto the enemy in force. We are ordered to be on the alert this evening; no countersign.

MONDAY, Feb. 15, 1864.

A chilly, cloudy morning but no wind; probably will snow before night. At 10 p. m. was ordered by Capt. H. R. Steele to take my command up to the reserve as soon as possible as the Johnnies were advancing in eight (whew!) different lines: think the man who reports this must be troubled with C. W. (commissary whiskey); arrived in camp at 4 p. m.; snowed all the afternoon. But what's become of the eight lines of C. W.?

Tuesday, Feb. 16, 1864.

Cloudy with a furious wind—in fact one of the most terrific gales of the winter —so piercing it's impossible to keep warm in our huts; have called on Mrs. G. E. Davis and Mrs. Ezra Stetson. All hands have been to prayer meeting this evening but me, and I have been studying; am stopping with Captain Samuel Darrah now; wind still high.

Wednesday, Feb. 17, 1864.

Clear and intensely cold, with high wind; have been studying in Dr. Almon Clark's quarters to-day; had a mock court-martial this evening at the chapel to entertain the ladies; sat up with Lieut. C. G. Newton till 1 a. m. Lieut. H. H. Dewey left for home this morning; no wind to-night, but very cold.

Thursday, Feb. 18, 1864.

Very cold but less wind than yesterday; had our monthly inspection this forenoon at ten o'clock; received no letter from home to-night. Dr. W. A. Child and wife have called this evening. He is a very bright, polished gentleman, but I am afraid of him; probably because he is older than I am; have been studying at Dr. Almon Clark's again to-day; wind abated but cold to-night.

Friday, Feb. 19, 1864.

Cold as ever but no wind to mention. Lieut E. P. Farr left for Vermont this morning; spent three hours this afternoon in the chapel with a class of non-commissioned officers who desire commissions in colored troops, and have requested me to hear them recite in tactics, etc., daily, before going before a board for examination in Washington, D. C. Received a letter from home; all well there. Carl Wilson is about entering a drug store in Montpelier, Vt.

Saturday, Feb. 20, 1864.

A very pleasant day but not warm. The men have been playing ball this afternoon; very dull otherwise; paymaster has come; have been very busy having men sign pay rolls. There is a detail for picket tomorrow, but I am not going.

Sunday, Feb. 21, 1864.

Cloudy, but no wind, threatening rain before night; regiment left for picket at 9 a. m.; very quiet in camp; religious services were held in the chapel at 4 p. m. by Rev. Mr. Parker of Waterbury, Vt. and a prayer service this evening, but I have not attended either. All's quiet.

MONDAY, Feb. 22, 1864.

Cloudy and warm. The Second Brigade was out drilling this forenoon as well as a battery; very busy this afternoon; paymaster paying off the regiment; rained a little this evening; got a paper from Vermont but don't know who sent it. There is a ball at First Corps headquarters to-night.

TUESDAY, Feb. 23, 1864.

A very pleasant day, but lonely in camp; dancing in the chapel this evening; moon shining brightly, and not a breath of air stirring, but for all this I can't study; no letters from home; all's quiet as midnight save the music in the chapel.

WEDNESDAY, Feb. 24, 1864.

Pleasant day with northwest wind. Col. A. B. Jewett and a select party have gone to Pony Mountain; picket guard came in about 4 p. m. First Corps had a review to-day, as well as the Second Corps; no letters from home; fine evening.

THURSDAY, Feb. 25, 1864.

Pleasant but windy. General French reviewed our division to-day—the Third of the Third Corps; muster and payrolls have come; after review spent three hours with my class at the chapel; reported the ladies will have to leave camp next week; hope it isn't so.

FRIDAY, Feb. 26, 1864.

Cloudy, high north wind but fair; air full of dust all day; had brigade drill this afternoon; dance in chapel this evening; General W. H. Morris present: Governor Smith has arrived in the army.

SATURDAY, Feb. 27, 1864.

Pleasant but chilly. The Sixth Corps is on the move this morning for Madison Court House—probably a reconnoissance. Governor Smith arrived in camp this forenoon. I started for picket about 4 p. m. to relieve the First Division of our Corps which is to accompany the Sixth Corps to Madison Court House; arrived on picket line at 2 a. m. Feb. 28.

SUNDAY, Feb. 28, 1864.

Did not get up till 9 a. m.; night march very fatiguing; not feeling well; cloudy and threatening rain. Captain P. D. Blodgett visited the line this morning; several Johnnies came into our lines this forenoon; everything quiet this evening.

MONDAY, Feb. 29, 1864.

Am feeling better this morning; weather gloomy; chilly south wind; considerable cannonading to-day towards Madison Court House; reported General Kilpatrick has captured a portion of Lee's picket line and penetrated to Orange Court House; pickets ordered to be vigilant, etc.

TUESDAY, March 1, 1864.

Commenced hailing about midnight and has continued to alternate with it and rain all day; trees and shubbery ice-covered and the day has been dismal; not as much cannonading as yesterday; relieved from picket about 6 p. m. by the Third Brigade; marched to camp on the pike.

WEDNESDAY, March 2, 1864.

Cleared during the night; ground covered with snow; weather fine; have been making out Lieut. Ezra Stetson's muster rolls; not with my class this afternoon; have nearly completed the second volume of tactics; no mail to-night.

THURSDAY, March 3, 1864.

The weather continues pleasant. Mrs. C. G. Chandler started for Vermont this morning. Mrs. Lieutenant-Colonel W. W. Henry arrived in camp this evening. Dr. Almon Clark has also arrived from Vermont. The Sixth Corps passed our camp this evening on its return from Madison Court House. General Kilpatrick has made a junction, it is said, with General B. F. Butler; camp very lonely to-night.

FRIDAY, March 4, 1864.

Weather calm and fine; no mud; pickets came in this afternoon; making muster and pay rolls; dance in chapel this evening; got a letter from Pert; has finished her school and all well at home. Lieutenant Thompson arrived in camp this morning.

SATURDAY, March 5, 1864.

Weather continues fine; completed B Company's muster and pay rolls this forenoon; Sutler George Skiff gave a ball in the chapel this evening; distinguished guests present; fine time. Dr. Child and wife called this evening, also Mrs. Hunt and Morse; no mail.

SUNDAY, March 6, 1864.

A beautiful day, no wind and quite warm. General W. H. Morris has had lady visitors from New York City. Our band has been playing for him. There were services to-day in the chapel; several ladies were present; good dress parade this evening; cheering news from Kilpatrick's cavalry.

MONDAY, March 7, 1864.

Very pleasant but colder than yesterday; have been hard at work all day with some men decorating the chapel with evergreens, etc.; got some help from the ladies; reception and dancing this evening. General J. B. Carr and lady were present and other distinguished guests. Captain Samuel Darrah was floor manager. Captain E. B. Frost looked after the supper; brilliant party.

TUESDAY, March 8, 1864.

It has been raining quite hard all day. The entertainment did not close last night till 2 a. m. to-day; have been returning the things borrowed for the hall last night; am feeling dull; no drill to-day; expect to be reviewed by General French to-morrow.

WEDNESDAY, March 9, 1864.

The weather has been very pleasant, but it's been a long weary day; have been at work on Company B clothing rolls, etc.; no recitation to-day. The Second Brigade has been having a review and drill this afternoon. The Third Corps review has been postponed till to-morrow, but I expected to go on picket; got a speech from Congressman Woodbridge; wonder what's come over him to be so civil; he's Meader's (my student roommate) law partner, but he was barely civil to me when I saw him in Vermont.

THURSDAY, March 10, 1864.

A lovely morning with a gentle south breeze; formed line at 9 a. m. for picket. Captain H. R. Steele in command of the detail from our brigade; commenced raining about 11 a. m. and continued all day. Our regiment is on the reserve. Lieutenant-Colonel Egbert of the Third Brigade, a fine man, is officer of the day.

FRIDAY, March 11, 1864.

It has rained hard all day. Lieut. J. S. Thompson and I have charge of the post on the pike. It is not a desirable one to be on, as the cavalry reserve is directly in front and they are continually passing and repassing, and the orders are very strict about passing anyone in or out of the lines. Colonel Ball is officer of the day and a good fellow.

SATURDAY, March 12, 1864.

It cleared during the night and it's fine this morning. I was on duty the last part of the night, but passed no one; wind blew furiously all day. A large party of citizens came through the lines destitute of nearly everything. A Colonel from the Third Brigade is officer of the day, and a strange fellow.

SUNDAY, March 13, 1864.

This is truly a fine day. A squadron of cavalry passed on the pike this morning to extend the cavalry picket line to Madison Court House; was relieved this afternoon by the Sixth Maryland Infantry; Major C. G. Chandler is officer of the day; arrived in camp about 5 p. m.; found Lieuts. Kingsley and Hill had returned from Vermont.

MONDAY, March 14, 1864.

Beautiful day. Most of the officers met at the hall this forenoon to make arrangements for another ball this evening; am on the committee to decorate the hall; have worked very hard all day, but am well repaid as all seem to be pleased with what I have done. Pretty decorations always add to the pleasure of all such gatherings. A large party was present.

TUESDAY, March 15, 1864.

Cold but pleasant; no wind; four hours' drill to-day, but I was excused being so busy at the chapel. I forgot to mention that Captain J. A. Sheldon returned from Vermont last night where he has been on recruiting service since November. The Third Corps is to be reviewed to-morrow by Major-General French.

WEDNESDAY, March 16, 1864.

Very cloudy and a high gale all day; formed line for review at 9 a. m.; moved a half mile out of camp, stacked arms, remained two hours and then started for the parade ground about a half mile away on John Minor Bott's farm; review passed off pleasantly, but it was very cold. The Corps made a fine appearance; wonder what Vermont people would think to see such a review; guess their eyes would pop plum out of their head.

THURSDAY, March 17, 1864.

The weather still continues boisterous. Hon. Portus Baxter's son arrived in camp last evening with several other Vermont gentlemen. They gave an entertainment at the Colonel's mess house this evening for the officers of the Tenth. I did not attend. Lieutenant E. P. Farr returned from Vermont this evening; received a letter from home.

FRIDAY, March 18, 1864.

Am not feeling well; took cold on review yesterday. The wind is blowing furiously, the air is full of dust, and it is a disgusting time. A party has gone to Pony Mountain. The long roll was beat and the regiment was hastily formed in line about 7 p. m. and so remained until 9 p. m. when it broke ranks. It was a scare. Such is army life in time of war.

SATURDAY, March 19, 1864.

The weather was truly fine this morning at sunrise, but about noon the wind blew a gale. Captain Samuel Darrah's Co. D of which I am second lieutenant challenged the regiment to play a game of ball for $50—or rather Captain Samuel Darrah did—which it accepted but lost the game. The regiment goes on picket to-morrow, but I don't expect to go. It looks like rain.

SUNDAY, March 20, 1864.

Clear and fine but rather cold. General W. H. Morris inspected the regiment this morning. A picket guard of two hundred and fifty men and eight officers left this morning. Captain J. A. Sheldon commanded the brigade detail. Services were held in the chapel at 4 p. m. Rev. Mr. Barnard of Williamstown, Vt. preached; weather cold.

MONDAY, March 21, 1864.

The weather continues fine but cold. General W. H. Morris inspected and reviewed the brigade. Preparations are being made for an army review; have been working on B Company's clothing rolls. Captain Samuel Darrah has gone over to division headquarters this evening. Captain Leonard, (Brigade Adjutant General), and Lieut. J. A. Hicks, A. D. C., have called. It's a beautiful evening.

TUESDAY, March 22, 1864.

The wind has blown furiously from the southeast all day. It's by far the most disagreeable day of the winter; commenced snowing about 5 p. m. and now at 11 p. m. there is eight inches on a level. My application to go before General Silas Casey's board for examination for a field office in colored troops has not been returned yet; shall put in another to-morrow.

WEDNESDAY, March 23, 1864.

Weather fine but very chilly. About eight inches of snow fell last night. Major C. G. Chandler is division officer of the day. A review of the army is expected in the course of two or three days. The army is anxiously waiting to see General U. S. Grant; sent in another application to go before General Silas Casey's board this evening; the pickets returned to-night.

THURSDAY, March 24, 1864.

Weather fine; some snow on the ground yet. Messrs. Smith and Farra arrived this evening from St. Albans, Vt. The regiment remained in line nearly all day in anticipation of General Grant's visit to the Army of the Potomac. A special train which he was probably on passed about 2 p. m. But what was the use of keeping troops under arms in line all day? It looks like C. W. again, or schoolboy management of which there is too much; got a letter from home tonight.

FRIDAY, March 25, 1864.

Chilly wind from the southeast; very cloudy; looks like rain; Company drill from 10 to 11 a. m. Our Third Division of the Third Corps has been permanently transferred as Third Division of the Sixth Corps, Brigadier-General Prince assuming command of the division. General French is ordered to Washington, D. C. Our regiment was a favorite with him, and the officers met in the chapel this evening to pass resolutions of regret, although we are glad to go to the gallant Sixth Corps if ours must be broken up.

SATURDAY, March 26, 1864.

It's a fine day; no wind; dull in camp; only ball playing for amusement which isn't half as exciting as being shot at by a Johnny. Our visitors from Vermont returned to St. Albans, Vt. this morning; services were held in the chapel this evening by Rev. Mr. Roberts of Williamstown, Vt.; weather fine.

SUNDAY, March 27, 1864.

It has been a beautiful day, warm and comfortable; snow all gone; wrote home, also to Captain G. W. Burnell; have not heard from my application yet. Chaplain E. M. Haynes preached a good sermon in the chapel this afternoon; good dress parade tonight; cloudy.

MONDAY, March 28, 1864.

It has been quite warm all day. The ladies started for home this morning but missed the train. We had a brigade review this forenoon, the first since we joined the Sixth Corps, and brigade dress parade in the evening which General Mead witnessed; picket in the morning.

TUESDAY, March 29, 1864.

An order came last night for us to move camp tomorrow. We hope it may be countermanded. The ladies started for Vermont this morning. Colonel A. B. Jewett went with them as far as Washington. A part of the regiment started for picket at 9 a. m.; has rained hard since 11 a. m.

WEDNESDAY, March 30, 1864.

It rained hard all night; didn't sleep a wink; got very wet; men in good spirits and everything working well in spite of the rain; have seen no officer of the day. Lieut. George P. Welch came down to see me this evening; very dark; camp quiet; looks like another storm before morning.

Thursday, March 31, 1864.

Weather quite agreeable to-day. The Lieutenant-Colonel of the One Hundred and Tenth Ohio Infantry is officer of the day, a very pleasant, agreeable man; think I should like him. The Third Division of our Corps has exchanged camp with our old First Division; have very poor quarters.

Friday, April 1, 1864.

A disappointing day; weather quite fine this morning; commenced raining about noon and has continued all day; was relieved from picket about 1 p. m. by the One Hundred and Thirty-eighth Pennsylvania Infantry; marched to the bridge the other side of Culpeper and waited for the officer of the day, but soon found to our disgust that he had gone to camp. He's no soldier! ought to be court-martialed!

Saturday, April 2, 1864.

Arrived in camp about dark last night and found the regiment in a mud hole without quarters fit to live in. How white men could be content to erect such winter quarters is beyond comprehension. Even the Johnnies do better. These quarters are the worst ever seen, besides being dirty. All are indignant and aggrieved at such ill treatment. It has rained or snowed hard all day to add to our discomfort; received a letter from C. B. Wilson and answered it; am disgusted about not being ordered before the Casey board for examination; fear I waited too long before making my application; probably have all the officers they want.

Sunday, April 3, 1864.

It has rained nearly all day; mud very deep in camp: more stormy weather the past two weeks than all winter before; most of the officers are building new cabins, the huts occupied by the previous regiment being uninhabitable. It's a dark and dismal camp, and very depressing.

Monday, April 4, 1864.

It has been a terrible day. The wind has blown a gale, it has snowed or rained incessantly all day, and we miss our old cabins greatly near Brandy Station. I have kept fairly comfortable, though. Such, however, is a soldier's life in the Army of the Potomac. It's a cold blustering evening without and were I not so busy studying I should be depressed and discontented.

TUESDAY, April 5, 1864.

The storm still continues, raged all night, and it was a tedious one; no order for Washington yet; alas! I fear I am doomed to disappointment all my life. Ah, well, so might it be, if it's God's will. Dick Moon arrived to-night direct from Vermont. I am glad to see him about again. It has ceased storming but the wind is still high.

WEDNESDAY, April 6, 1864.

Cloudy and windy this morning, but it cleared up about noon; fine evening, too, but no moon; have been over to the theatre, but hardly got paid for my trouble except for the novelty of seeing a theatre built of logs. It is as big as a city theatre, is of fine rustic work and a curiosity. It was built by the Engineers and is handsome. Of course in a big army like this there is plenty of fair theatrical talent and some excellent. The band came out this evening and played a few pieces, the first with their new instruments; am at work on Company B clothing rolls; will finish in about two days.

THURSDAY, April 7, 1864.

Muddy under foot, but sunshiny and warm; received a letter from home; all well there; have not been very busy to-day; men working hard building cabins in the new camp four or five hundred yards away; will probably complete it in season to break camp in when the spring campaign opens. It's a handsome camp, every cabin being exactly alike, commodious and is symmetrically laid out, the handsomest I ever saw. But the Tenth Vermont leads the army in such a way and is the pride of general officers from army headquarters down; it is just the same in drill, parade, forced marching, fighting or any place it is put. The men have great *esprit de corps*, and strive not to be outdone by any other regiment in anything. Were it not that the men's minds are kept occupied, I should doubt the expediency of putting so much work into a new camp so late in the season, but they seem to enjoy it, so it's all right; it keeps them healthy and hard, too; besides, they will be in splendid shape for the campaign close at hand; there's no moon to-night but it's beautiful starlight; bands are serenading at division headquarters. In the stillness of the night the distance softens the splendid music and makes it enchanting. I sit outside alone in deep thought and dream over it. War is such a strange companion!

FRIDAY, April 8, 1864.

Weather warm and pleasant the fore part of the day, but towards night it hazed up; probably will rain to-morrow; had a long and tiresome brigade drill this afternoon that disgusted everybody, and I think a useless one; received my order from the Secretary of War to report to General Silas Casey's board; shall not go till Tuesday.

SATURDAY, April 9, 1864.

My predictions are fully realized, it has rained torrents all day; haven't done a thing but mope over the fire; so muddy outside it's almost impossible to get round even if it didn't rain so; have sent in an application for three days' leave to go to Washington for examination; very busy reviewing tactics; no letters.

SUNDAY, April 10, 1864.

Storm has ceased, but it's muddy and windy; part of the regiment started for picket this morning. Lieut. Ezra Stetson has gone so I will be alone; have been studying all day; Sergeant J. M. Reed called this evening, also Dick who will stay all night, his quarters being crowded; rather dull in camp all day.

MONDAY, April 11, 1864.

Rested finely last night; weather fair; had a three hours' brigade drill this afternoon; proved more of a march than a drill; regiment very small owing to so many being on detached service, and on other details; men busy, too, on their log cabins in the new camp. Dick is with me to-night; think he prefers being where he isn't so much crowded as in his own quarters.

TUESDAY, April 12, 1864.

Weather comfortable and warm, but few clouds and very little wind. If the weather still continues fine a few days longer the army will make an advance without doubt; have been talking with our sutler's clerk, Huntington, who was a lieutenant in the rebel army thirteen months, but being a Vermonter, on the death of his wife and child who were living in the south, he deserted to our army.

WEDNESDAY, April 13, 1864.

Warm and comfortable; mud drying up finely; application to go to Washington to report to General Silas Casey returned this forenoon, disapproved; had a brigade drill this afternoon, a better one than usual; men busy on their cabins; wish they were done as their present ones are very filthy; a beautiful moonlight night.

THURSDAY, April 14, 1864.

Weather fine, no wind or clouds and but little mud; had our regimental monthly inspection at 10 a. m.; have written to Major Fostor, Chief of Bureau for the Organization of U. S. C. T. in regard to appearing before the Casey board for examination; no letter from home to-night; several callers this evening.

FRIDAY, April 15, 1864.

Weather fine this forenoon but began to cloud up towards night. Major Harper has paid off the regiment to-day. The sutler is also selling off his stock of goods, as to-morrow is the time appointed for all sutlers to leave the army; looks like a move in a few days; am detailed for picket to-morrow; no letter from home to-night, am sorry to say.

SATURDAY, April 16, 1864.

Corps review was ordered for to-day, but it is raining, so very likely it will be postponed; started for picket about 9 a. m. with Col. W. W. Henry as Officer of the Day, so we will fare well; rained all forenoon; cleared about 1 p. m.; fair since. The Tenth Vermont has the right of the line.

SUNDAY, April 17, 1864.

Weather fine and warm, but some windy with clouds; all quiet along the line to-day; have very poor quarters; has been very quiet in front; it's doubtless the calm which precedes the storm; have little doubt but what the army will move within the next week; beautiful, moonlight, calm evening; it seems ominous.

MONDAY, April 18, 1864.

It has been very comfortable on picket to-day without any fire. The officer of the day has been at my post to-day for the first time. Generals Grant, Meade and Sedgwick, are reviewing the Sixth Corps to-day; regret not being present. One of the bough houses caught fire this evening and burned up; otherwise all's quiet.

TUESDAY, April 19, 1864.

The weather is getting uncomfortably warm; no need of fire any more on picket. A skirmish occurred last night about fifteen miles out on the pike. One or two of the enemy were killed and as many wounded. One of our men was wounded in the foot. A detachment of our cavalry came in this morning with some prisoners.

WEDNESDAY, April 20, 1864.

Not very pleasant to-day; brigade drill this forenoon; regiment so busy putting up quarters it is excused from all other duties; officers of Tenth Vermont all ordered out to witness the new movements in tactics at brigade drill. My leave has come back approved, but shan't go to Washington till Sunday; clear moonlight night.

THURSDAY, April 21, 1864.

A truly beautiful day, warm and pleasant with no wind at all; regiment moved to a new camp this morning; most of the line officers remain here yet. The three left Companies, B, G and K contested for the medal Major C. G. Chandler proposed giving last winter, and B, my old Company and the one I have been with all winter, won it. Of course it would! It always honors itself and me; got a letter from home to-night.

FRIDAY, April 22, 1864.

Weather pleasant and agreeable this morning, but towards night it began to haze up and now it is sprinkling. A part of the regiment went on picket this morning. Major Chandler is officer of the day; had a dress parade to-night. Lieut. J. A. Hicks is relieved from General W. H. Morris' staff. Most of the line officers have moved over to the new camp.

SATURDAY, April 23, 1864.

It cleared during the night; quite fair this morning, but by noon the wind blew a gale, and the air was loaded with dust and smoke, but the sun was shining; shall start for Washington in the morning; have written Dr. Jones to-night. It's lonely and I'm feeling depressed.

SUNDAY, April 24, 1864.

It's been a beautiful day; left camp at 6 o'clock this morning and reached Brandy Station at 9 a. m. One would hardly think it was Sunday by the stir about camp and our base of supplies, but war knows no Sunday; arrived in Washington at 4 p. m. and went to the National Hotel. War rumors load the very air here.

MONDAY, April 25, 1864.

It has been a pleasant spring day; reported to General Silas Casey this morning: will be examined tomorrow; sat at Bradey's this afternoon for pictures. The streets are thronged with moving bodies of troops. General Burnside's Corps passed through the city this afternoon. President Lincoln reviewed it from the balcony over the ladies' entrance of Willard's Hotel on Fourteenth street. This is my first sight of President Lincoln and probably as good as I shall ever have. I was just across the street opposite on the curb and not crowded. He looked pale, very sad and greatly careworn. It depressed me to look at him. The remembrance will ever be vivid. Burnside's Corps has encamped near Alexandria for the night; saw Othello played at Grover's Theatre tonight (now the New National).

TUESDAY, April 26, 1864.

Fine day. Several regiments have passed up Pennsylvania Avenue during the day; have been before the board; am very much pleased with its appearance with the exception of General Silas Casey who is too old and childish for such business. To my surprise I was asked what position I wanted, and I replied a field office; was told the supply was more than the demand and as officers were absorbed in the same order as passed by the board I would never be called on. I replied that I should never accept anything but a field office; was passed for a first class Captaincy, there being three grades, First, Second and Third class; saw Edwin Forrest play Mattamora tonight at Ford's Theatre. It was fine.

WEDNESDAY, April 27, 1864.

Pleasant but some wind; started for the front on the 9 a. m. train; passed General Burnside's Corps south of Alexandria en route towards Ft. Albany; arrived in camp about sundown; found everything as I left it; am with my own Company (D) now, Lieut. J. A. Hicks having returned to Company B, which is his own company.

THURSDAY, April 28, 1864.

A part of the regiment went on picket this morning; am officer of the day. I forgot to mention that on my return I was surprised to find that Col. A. B. Jewett had resigned and that his resignation had been accepted; received a letter from Capt. Albert F. Dodge and one from home tonight; have been very busy making out muster and pay rolls all day.

FRIDAY, April 29, 1864.

It has been warm and pleasant; nothing going on in camp; men seem to be enjoying themselves playing ball; completed Company D muster and pay rolls. Lieut. G. P. Welch relieved me this morning as officer of the day. Capt. E. B. Frost is now acting Major; very dull in camp tonight. Colonel W. W. Henry is division officer of the day.

SATURDAY, April 30, 1864.

Weather uncomfortably warm this forenoon but cooler since. Major C. G. Chandler mustered the regiment this forenoon; no drill this afternoon. General Burnside's Corps has relieved the Fifth Corps which has been doing duty on the railroad. The Third Division has moved in on our left; all's quiet tonight.

SUNDAY, May 1, 1864.

Weather fine and pleasant. Major C. G. Chandler made a thorough inspection of the regiment this morning. Lieutenant Clark from the sharpshooters called on me this afternoon; pickets came in about 4 o'clock. Chaplain E. M. Haynes preached a good sermon today; have written to J. R. Seaver.

MONDAY, May 2, 1864.

Still another fine day, and yet the army remains idle. The query generally is, "when will the army move, and where?" I guess we will wish it hadn't when it does move. General U. S. Grant seems to keep his own counsel, like the silent man he is. It is well. A furious wind-storm occurred about 5 o'clock p. m. but did not disturb us much.

Tuesday, May 3, 1864.

Pleasant in the forenoon, but a gale this afternoon; had brigade drill two hours this afternoon. At last our query for the past two weeks has been answered. A part of the army moved to-day, and no doubt we shall go to-morrow; received orders at 6 o'clock p. m. to march at 4 o'clock a. m. to-morrow. All is confusion in camp.

Wednesday, May 4, 1864.

We were aroused this morning at 3 o'clock, formed line at daylight, and took up our line of march for Germania Ford about sunrise. The whole army is evidently on the move. It looks more like business than ever before; arrived at the ford about 6 o'clock p. m.; found that our cavalry crossed here last night without opposition; are encamped on the south side of the river not over fifty yards from it.

Thursday, May 5, 1864.

Pleasant and warm; remained at the fort until about 8 o'clock a. m. waiting for General Burnside's forces to relieve us, and then marched about two miles up the plank road and formed line of battle in a piece of woods to the right of the road; remained here until noon when Burnside's corps again came up and occupied our line when we pushed on to the front passing many corralled and moving army trains, and through the outskirts of the field hospital near the right of our army's infantry line of battle until we struck the Orange turnpike when we turned to the right and followed it some distance until near enough the enemy to draw the fire of its artillery when seemingly the air was full of solid shot and exploding shells as far each side the pike as could be seen. The road here ran in a straight line ahead of us almost as far as the eye could reach bordered on either side with a dense forest and underbrush which was also being shelled in places. Shortly after, when within shelling distance, the enemy fired a solid shot straight along the pike which tore screeching through the air just a little above the heads of the men in column in our regiment till it struck the pike about midway the regiment, providentially where the men had split and were marching on either side of the road, when it viciously rebounded along the pike lengthwise the column to the great consternation of the men all along the extended column in our own and other regiments. This situation was most trying for every moment I dreaded the effect of a better directed shot which would go destructively through our long column lengthwise and do untold damage.

Soon, however, we turned to the left or southerly into the woods and formed line of battle almost as soon as there was room after leaving the road with the enemy close in our front with a field piece of artillery hardly a hundred yards away through the brush which kept each from seeing the other. Before Captain H. R. Steele had hardly finished dressing his company after forming line a shell from this gun exploded in the ranks of Company K, killing a private and wounding others. The shell had burst actually inside the man completely disemboweling and throwing him high in the air in a rapidly whirling motion above our heads with arms and legs extended until his body fell heavily to the ground with a sickening thud.

I was in the line of file closers hardly two paces away and just behind the man killed. We were covered with blood, fine pieces of flesh, entrails, etc., which makes me cringe and shudder whenever I think of it. The concussion badly stunned me. I was whirled about in the air like a feather, thrown to the ground on my hands and knees—or at least was in that position with my head from the enemy when I became fully conscious—face cut with flying gravel or something else, eyes, mouth and ears filled with dirt, and was feeling nauseated from the shake-up. Most of the others affected went to the hospital, and I wanted to but didn't give up. I feared being accused of trying to get out of a fight.

The Division Commander and staff were about three hundred yards more or less, behind us in direct line with this gun that was shelling us. Another shell from it which went screeching close over us—for we immediately after the first shot lay flat on the ground—disemboweled Captain G. B. Damon's horse of the Tenth Vermont on the Division staff, on which he was mounted, and killed two others. This party could be seen from where I was in line plainly. I was surprised at the quickness with which Company K got into line again after being so disrupted by the exploding shell in its ranks.

Friday, May 6, 1864.

We slept on our arms last night. Report says that we forced the enemy's right flank back about three miles yesterday besides capturing a goodly number of prisoners, but I doubt it. It is also rumored that the Vermont Brigade of our Corps was badly cut up yesterday afternoon, but I hope it's not true; it was hotly engaged, though, on our left. We were led further off into the woods this forenoon to form another line of battle evidently, but General Seymour who was in charge seemed to be dazed, and while poking around alone in front of and too far away from his command without a skirmish line in his front, was taken prisoner. A part of our brigade was finally detached and taken north of and just to the right of the Orange turnpike including our regiment where we formed line behind some natural breastworks with the enemy's earthworks about fifty yards more or less in our front across a pretty, level, green field, in the edge of the woods; this work of theirs was in front, I am told, of the enemy's main line. We were shelled more or less at times through the day until about mid-afternoon when we were let alone.

Later in the day all at once hearing heavy firing on the right flank of our army not far away, Colonel W. W. Henry excitedly called us to attention, faced us to the right and then turning the head of the column directly to the rear we ran with all speed possible—there was no double quick about it—for a mile or more into the woods in rear of where the heavy firing on our right was, stumbling over logs, ditches, brush, etc., till our faces, hands and shins smarted from bruises and scratches, when we were halted all out of breath, faced to the left and ordered to give the charging war cry which, being a good deal wrought up, not knowing what had happened but that a disaster had occurred to our forces as panic-stricken men were hastening to the rear from our defeated right through our lines, and not knowing our own position relatively speaking to any other of our forces, or but what we would be pounced upon any moment, for we had but a small part of our brigade even, with us, so far as I could see in the woods, and annihilated, we, together with the One Hundred and Sixth New York Volunteer Infantry and Fourteenth New Jersey repeatedly gave the war cry as we had never given it before or did give it again afterwards. It reverberated again and again in the forest until the echo died away in the gloaming as softly as a fond mother's lullaby, and it pleased me at the time to think that perhaps it was God's offering through us and the medium of nature, or His lullaby to the thousands of wounded and dying heroes both of the blue and the grey within hearing, for the softly dying echoes certainly were soothing and restful in the quiet twilight even to me. This war cry had the effect not only to stop the enemy's firing but its advance, thinking probably it was a counter-assault to meet theirs, and it saved many a poor fellow from being captured, as the enemy ceased its aggressive tactics in order to reform and be prepared to meet our anticipated assault.

General Jubal A. Early's Division of three brigades had stolen round in rear of General Shaler's veteran brigade of the First Division and the Second Brigade (formerly General Seymour's) of green men of the Third Division, Sixth Corps, which were on the right of our army in the order mentioned, attacked vigorously both in rear and front, threw Shaler's veterans into disorder as well later as the Second Brigade, captured Shaler and created temporary confusion among the trains and hospital corps nearby. Seemingly it was the result of bad generalship by someone on our side. If I had been a General in command there, I'll bet the Johnnies wouldn't have got away with me! It was evidently lack of alertness, and the Johnny fellow got the best of it because the most alert.

Generals Meade and Sedgwick probably returning from an investigation of that part of the battlefield after the fight just after dark near our regiment where I was, inquired what troops were there and on being told it was the Tenth Vermont at that particular point Sedgwick said to Meade, "We are safe enough with that regiment!" as though they doubted the security of their surroundings.

S<small>ATURDAY</small>, May 7, 1864.

Weather very warm, but suited to the work we have got to do. We fell back about a half mile last night, just after Generals Meade and Sedgwick passed our regiment, to some breastworks in which we lay on our arms all night. This morning we were moved to a stronger position on a ridge just to the left of the position we occupied last night, and threw up very strong breastworks, several brass cannon having been placed along the ridge before our arrival. We have remained as support to this artillery all day, but it hasn't been used. The enemy made an attempt to carry the works to our left on the pike early this morning but were repulsed in less than five minutes with a loss of two hundred. We have remained on the defensive all day. The Second Corps repulsed the enemy just at dark, as it was trying to carry their works.

Our regiment has not been engaged to-day, but the suspense has been wearing. The rebel yell when they have made their various assaults at other places on the line to our left, and the ominous bull-dog-like silence along our lines till the roar of musketry commenced when the enemy got in range, made one at the time almost breathless and his heart to stand still on any part of the line. It is awful! But the rebel yell makes one clinch his teeth and determine that it shall be victory for us or death before we will give up our works. But I don't like war and wish it was well over. This is the *real* thing, though! Grant don't *play* fight.

Our casualties in the Wilderness including the Ninth Corps were 10,220 wounded, 2,902 missing, and 2,265 killed, making a total of 15,387. The Confederate loss was 6,000 wounded, 3,400 missing, and 2,000 killed, making a total of 11,400. The Tenth Vermont lost nine wounded and three killed.

S<small>UNDAY</small>, May 8, 1864.

It has been *very* warm and sultry. Our forces commenced a flank movement last night. We withdrew from the enemy's front about 10 o'clock p. m. and marched, via the Chancellorsville turnpike—where we passed many trains, our wounded and Burnside's Corps—through the old battlefield of Chancellorsville of a year ago, as far as Piney Branch Church, when we left the pike at Alsop's house, and after marching southerly some time on the Todd's Tavern road formed line of battle near Alsop's farm about 3 o'clock p. m., our Division being on the right of the Sixth Corps. We advanced across the Ny river—a mere creek—but meeting with a sharp artillery fire from a rebel battery on the opposite ridge to us skirting the valley, we were ordered to halt. This was about three miles north of Spottsylvania Court House and is called the Battle of Alsop's Farm. Our regiment lost sixteen men here. Generals Robinson and Griffin's Divisions of the Fifth Corps took two thousand prisoners and lost about one thousand.

We continued to change position from one point to another till just after passing Spottsylvania when just before dark we found the enemy in our front in force. It had felled trees across the road which delayed us considerably, but our artillery soon opened the way for us. We proceeded about two miles and found the enemy strongly intrenched across an open slightly rising field from us in the edge of the woods which was fiercely charged by us but without effect except to be repulsed with the field covered largely with our killed and badly wounded. General Meade was in rear of our regiment which formed a rear line in our assaulting column, superintending the assault, and when jocularly reminded by a wag that he (Meade) was in a dangerous place, he graciously replied: "It's safe enough behind a Vermont regiment anywhere!" Which was a clever thing to say to the men and they appreciated it. We threw up breastworks after the assault, uncomfortably close to the enemy and are well fortified, but not in as naturally a strong position as the enemy. Assaulting in the dark is unsatisfactory and very demoralizing. It ought not to be done when it can be avoided, one is so apt to shoot his own men and straggle into the enemy's lines and be captured; it's very trying and nerve-taxing. It has been a strenuous day.

Monday, May 9, 1864.

Our army's line is about five miles long this morning and runs northwest by southeast. General Hancock occupies the right followed by General Warren, Generals Sedgwick and Burnside in the order mentioned. Our batteries have been shelling the enemy fiercely all day and this evening, but the heaviest fighting seems to be on our left. Our regiment was terribly shelled when supporting batteries which has been all day. We were ordered to lie flat on the ground in one instant and there's no doubt but what we did for the ground was a dead level and the shells whistled and shrieked very thickly and closely over us. It was *terribly* nerve-trying. The Johnnies didn't want to see us bad enough though, to come over and call. We could see many dead between the lines in our front a little to the left of where we supported a battery this morning, of both armies, as a result of the assault last night. It is a shocking sight, but such is war.

TUESDAY, May 10, 1864.

Warm and sultry. The stench from the dead between the lines is terrible. There has been hard fighting on our right all day. As for the Tenth Vermont it has been supporting a battery most of the time. According to rumor we have captured a large number of prisoners and several pieces of artillery. About 6 o'clock p. m. our batteries opened a tremendous fire on the enemy's works, and kept it up for two hours, but with what result I do not know, except that the guns in our front were silenced. It was a fine artillery duel and the roar appalling even to a practiced ear. We are getting the best of Lee in this battle but it's stubborn fighting on both sides.

The accuracy with which our gunners fire is wonderful. I have seen one piece of the enemy's artillery opposite me turned completely over backwards carriage and all, by a solid shot from one of our guns in front of our regiment; it evidently hit the enemy's cannon square in the muzzle. It is awe-inspiring to see the regularity, the determined set look and precision with which our begrimed artillerymen stick to their work; shot and shell screeching close by don't seem to disturb them. I was spellbound and speechless with awe and admiration for their splendid pluck and nerve for some time, at first. No words can picture such a scene. I'd rather be a "doughboy" though—anything but an artilleryman, for I hate shells and solid shot. I think I can face anything in a charge without flinching after this splendid exhibition of nerve.

Our regiment relieved the One Hundred and Fifty-first Ohio Volunteer Infantry on the skirmish line to-night. I am on lookout in a grave-like hole about the length of a man some two feet deep on top of a hillock with cut bushes stuck all about as a mask in the soft dirt thrown from the hole. The cheerfully suggestive grave-like hole is wide enough for two, and I have Corporal Shedd with me. Even such a place is *fine* under the circumstances for there is a constant whizzing of bullets and shrieking shells over my abode. We are not more than fifty yards from our main line so close are the two armies at this point. We have to relieve each other at night stealthily under the cover of darkness.

WEDNESDAY, May 11, 1864.

Very sultry until about 5 o'clock p. m. when the heavens became shrouded with dark and threatening clouds and a terrific thunder-storm followed, which continued till about dark, when our whippoorwill again dolefully sang out "Whip-em-well! Whip-em-well!" as our men are pleased to interpret it. A whippoorwill has appeared midway between the lines every evening since we left winter camp, with its solemn song, until the men regard it as a good omen. It don't seem to occur to them that the enemy may regard it the same way, as meant for them to whip us.

There has been a furious cannonading kept up by our side all day. The enemy has made three or four fruitless attempts to plant batteries, and return the fire in our front, but without success; has been hard fighting on our left all day by the rest of the Sixth Corps and General Hancock's men; was relieved from my pit by Lieut. G. E. Davis. I ache all over from having been in the hole twenty-four hours in the same position. It wasn't safe to stand up nor did I try it, as it would draw the sharpshooter's fire up the trees, etc. One could only occasionally raise his head high enough to peek under the bushes, during lulls in firing, which masked our position as the place was almost continually under fire. It is close by on the ground occupied by our regiment and in its front that General Sedgwick, our Corps Commander, was killed by a sharpshooter when locating a battery, and where General W. H. Morris, our Brigade Commander was wounded when changing the position of two regiments which makes us doubly cautious. It's a dangerous point being high and furthest advanced of any part of the line. The stench from the dead is sickening and terrible.

THURSDAY, May 12, 1864.

Rained all night and incessantly till 10 o'clock a. m. There has been desperate fighting by the Sixth and Second Corps on our left all day at the "Bloody Angle" where they have held the enemy back as well as tried to take its works, but with great loss of life. This will evidently go down as one of the most bloody and desperate battles of the war. The Tenth Vermont was relieved by some of the Fifth Corps about 3 o'clock p. m., our Division having been ordered further to the left adjoining the "Bloody Angle" or "Slaughter Pen." Just after we had stacked arms under the brow of a slight ridge next the bloody angle, Captain H. R. Steele wandered a little distance in front and almost immediately returned hopping along holding up his foot saying he was shot. I ordered some of the men to take him to the hospital.

I am now in command of Company K. The men seem pleased, and I'm sure I am for I like the Company. The men seem sensible, and I know them to be reliable good fighters. I am not sure but what they will win my esteem from Company B, but I never have been fickle; there's room in my heart for all the men of the gallant old Tenth Vermont. They have faith in me and it's mutual. They will never be turned down by me. We are to bivouac on our arms in a dense growth of pine forest with the enemy immediately a short distance in front. *Surely* this fierce struggle of giant armies can't last more than a day more. Either one or the other will have to yield, and as we have had the best of it here thus far, it will be Lee.

It is wet and depressing for the "Slaughter Pen" will be our portion next without Lee withdraws to-night which God grant he may do if it is His will. The thought that we may have to assault into the jaws of death at the bloody angle in the gray of the morning is appalling for I am told there are thousands of dead and uncared for wounded on the field between the lines, and in the rebel works the dead and wounded lay in piles, the wounded bound in by the dead several deep. The rattle and roar of musketry and artillery is dreadful as I write and may continue all night. I am about to lie down perhaps for my last sleep, but I'm too exhausted to have the thought keep me awake for seldom has sleep, sweet sleep, been more welcome. But I have never thought I should be killed in battle. It's delightful to have perfect faith—the faith of a child in such a way. It helps one to go into battle, although I dread being wounded, it shocks the system so. I never go into a fight or take a railroad journey, though, without feeling reconciled to yield up my spirit to Him who gave it if it is His will. This gives one calmness and reconciliation unspeakable. God be praised for giving me such peace. This is my prayer.

FRIDAY, May 13, 1864.

My prayer for Lee's withdrawal last night was granted. Our Division moved to the "Bloody Angle" this morning; it virtually joined our regiment's left last night. The enemy abandoned the angle during the night after three days' *desperate* fighting. No pen can fully describe the appearance of the battlefield—and yet our wounded and dead have been cared for, and some of the enemy's, by us and *such* are mostly out of view. The sight of the enemy's dead is something dreadful. There are *three* dead lines of battle a half mile more or less in length—men killed in every conceivable manner. The wounded are fairly bound in by the dead. Lee abandoned his works leaving most of his wounded, and all his dead in our hands unburied. Several pieces of artillery were taken. Prisoners say that General Lee fought in person as it meant the loss of his army if his line was broken here, as well as Richmond.

No wonder from its present appearance this place has been christened the "Bloody Angle" and the "Slaughter Pen." For several hundred yards—fully a half mile or more—in the edge of the heavy oak forest of immense trees skirting an open field, the enemy's works are faultlessly strong of large oak logs and dirt shoulder high with traverses fifty feet back every sixty feet or so. This breastwork is filled with dead and wounded where they fell, several deep nearly to the top in front, extending for forty feet more or less back gradually sloping from front to rear, to one deep before the ground can be seen. The dead as a whole as they lie in their works are like an immense wedge with its head towards the works. Think of such a mass of dead! hundreds and hundreds piled top of each other! At the usual distance in rear of these breastworks—about ninety feet—are two more complete dead lines of battle about one hundred feet apart the dead bodies lying where the men fell in line of battle shot dead in their tracks. The lines are perfectly defined by dead men so close they touch each other. Many of the bodies have turned black, the stench is terrible, and the sight shocking beyond description. I saw several wounded men in the breastworks buried under their dead, just move a hand a little as it stuck up through the interstices above the dead bodies that buried the live ones otherwise completely from sight. Imagine such a sight if one can! It is indescribable! It was sickening, distressing and shocking to look upon! But, above all, think if one can of the feelings of the brave men who, regiment after regiment, were marched up in line of battle time and again for several days to fight with such a sight confronting them! Could anything in Hades be any worse? Only the misery I imagine, of an uneasy conscience at some great wrong done an innocent person could exceed it. It seems like a horrible nightmare! Such intrepidity is worthy of a better cause. Was there ever before such a shocking battlefield? Will the historian ever correctly record it? No pen can do it. The sight of such a horror *only* can fully portray it.

The First and Second Divisions of the Sixth Corps and Hancock's men have done most of the fighting today at the "Bloody Angle." The Sixth Corps has lost eight hundred and forty wounded and two hundred and fifty killed. The loss of our army at Spottsylvania Court House has been five thousand two hundred and thirty-three of which number nine hundred have been killed. Our Division has lost in this fight to-day twenty-three killed and one hundred and twenty-three wounded. I examined this forenoon an oak tree fully eighteen inches in diameter felled by being cut off by minie bullets at the apex of the "Bloody Angle" occupied by the enemy. I could hardly believe my eyes, but there stood the stump and the felled tree with the wood for two feet or more all eaten away by bullets.

SATURDAY, May 14, 1864.

We were aroused several times during the night by sharp firing on the skirmish line. About daylight we received an order to move further to the left, and soon found ourselves on the extreme flank of the old line of battle. Soon after we left our old position, the skirmish line that had caused us so much trouble during the night was captured. We found on examination that Lee's army fell back during the night still further. We moved about two miles towards Spottsylvania Court House, charged across the valley and Ny river, and took possession of the heights where Lee's headquarters were this morning relieving the First Division of our Corps which had been hotly engaged. Thus we virtually part with the stage on which was fought one of the greatest battles of modern times if not in history, and no one regrets it; it seems like a horrible dream. But how about the uneasy souls—the remorse of those who are responsible for this war in the hereafter? What does it all mean, anyway? Is man irresponsible? Should he not have a care? Verily!

SUNDAY, May 15, 1864.

Cloudy, with a bracing air; have thrown up a line of rifle pits along our front. The army is quiet to-day; very little cannonading heard. Divine services were held in nearly every regiment in the Brigade; wrote to Pert this forenoon. The Sixth Corps is encamped on as beautiful a plantation as I ever saw. It seems a pity to spoil such finely laid out grounds, but such is war. The whole Division got ready to move about 6 o'clock a. m. but as the enemy remained quiet we did. There's no picket firing to-night. I'm so tired and lousy I do wish we could stay somewhere long enough to wash and boil our underclothing. However, the general officers are as lousy as the rest of us for lice in war times know no caste. I saw a General lousing to-day. I hope this won't shock anyone when they read it after I have passed along. It's a part of the history of the civil war though, and should be recorded.

Monday, May 16, 1864.

It was sultry and warm until 4 o'clock p. m. when relief came through a fierce thunder-storm; no fighting; remained quietly in camp all day; much appreciated mail came to-night; got two letters from Pert, one from Abby and one from Dr. J. H. Jones. I know not how long we shall remain in this position, but God grant that this suspense will soon be ended. I dread another such battle as that of last week and hope we may avoid one for a while, anyway.

Tuesday, May 17, 1864.

Cloudy with wind; regiment has been on the skirmish line; have advanced about a mile by swinging our left round nearly parallel with our present line of battle; met with no opposition; enemy seems to be in the valley between the two flanks of our army; no news to-day; army very quiet; can't continue long, as Grant seems to be cautiously working round both flanks of the enemy; things look suspicious to-night; mistrust something's afoot.

Wednesday, May 18, 1864.

We were ordered to withdraw our line this morning at 3 o'clock which we did without difficulty; found our Corps had gone to the extreme right of the line to reinforce the Second Corps, quite a little brush having occurred between it and the enemy this morning which was repulsed and driven back into the valley; occupy the same ground we did yesterday; have orders to march in the morning at daylight; another mail came this evening; all's quiet. Perly Farrer was killed to-day on the skirmish line. He was a good boy, a member of my old Company B, of which I am so proud and fond. His remains will be numbered with the unknown dead, as it will be impossible to send them north now. He was a brave man and died manfully doing his whole duty. We can't even reach his body now.

Thursday, May 19, 1864.

We were ready according to orders to march early this morning. General Burnside moved his Corps to the left of us during the night. We all moved about a mile and a half to the left and threw up a new line of entrenchments: enemy about twelve hundred yards in our front; weather fine; small shower about 5 o'clock p. m. cooled the air greatly; enemy quiet in our front, but heard heavy guns about dark on the extreme left; don't know the cause or result.

Friday, May 20, 1864.

Weather very warm and sultry; showery towards night; enemy in front all day; neither side seem ready for another fight at present; no picket firing to-day to mention. General Meade rode along the line and seemed much pleased with our breastworks; said if we could hold them eight days we should be all right; don't know what he meant by this; mail to-day; all's quiet.

Saturday, May 21, 1864.

Very warm and sultry until about 5 o'clock p. m. when quite a hard thunderstorm come up and cooled off the air; remained in our breastworks until about 4 o'clock p. m. when the first line was abandoned for the second where we remained about an hour when all withdrew. Our Division was in rear and had not gone more than twenty-five rods from our works when the rebs charged on our picket line but without effect in our front, except to make us double quick back and reoccupy our intrenchments where we remained about two hours then quietly withdrew and marched all night. It's been a worrying day. Since the fourteenth we've done nothing but march and countermarch and change about.

Sunday, May 22, 1864.

The enemy appeared on our right flank about 3 o'clock a. m. evidently with the intention of cutting us off from the rest of the army, but didn't succeed. It has been very warm all day, and by far the most difficult marching we have had during the campaign; encamped near Bowling Green. General Hancock is reported ten miles ahead of us; no fighting to-day.

Monday, May 23, 1864.

We were ordered to be in readiness to march at 4 o'clock this morning, but did not start till near 9 o'clock a. m.; marched until about 11 o'clock a. m., and encamped about three miles from the North Anna river; heavy artillery firing heard in the direction of the river; have not heard the result; very warm all day, but the men bear the heat grandly. General Longstreet's Corps is only about three miles ahead of us from which it would seem we are chasing him— anyway, have captured many of his stragglers. It's intensely hot.

Tuesday, May 24, 1864.

The weather continues very warm, but thanks to the citizens along our line of march for their ice houses we are doing very well by helping ourselves to such needed comforts as happen to be in sight. Probably they would rather the Johnnies should have them, but they are on their last legs—they are playing out. We broke camp this morning about 6 o'clock a. m.; arriving at the North Anna river about 10 o'clock a. m.; found the Fifth Corps had crossed last night after a hard artillery duel which was what we heard. We crossed the river at Jericho Mills and laid on the south side of the river until 6 o'clock p. m., and then moved to the left to reinforce General Russell; saw General U. S. Grant to-day for the first time, at his mess table under a tent fly; was in his shirtsleeves; good view. The men enjoyed the bathing this afternoon greatly. The whole army seemingly has been in swimming. At any rate I never saw so many in bathing at once before or those who seemed to enjoy it more. It was a sight to be remembered. We marched towards the South Anna river till 8 o'clock p. m. when we ran into the enemy's pickets, fell back a little, camped and threw up breastworks.

Wednesday, May 25, 1864.

It has been a very warm day, but we have not had to march much; laid on our arms in line of battle last night behind our works at Quarles' Mills; no skirmishing in front till this morning. A portion of the Sixth Corps passed by us to the left and ran into the enemy a few rods beyond. Our brigade started about 10 o'clock a. m. and marched to Noles Station as did the First Division of our Corps. We burned the depot, destroyed the Virginia Central Railroad for about seven miles, and returned to the train; remained there about an hour, changed position to the left about two miles and camped for the night.

Thursday, May 26, 1864.

We were ordered on picket last night; no appearance of any enemy in our front; men enjoying the novelty of foraging greatly; rained hard about an hour this morning and has been cloudy and gloomy all day; has been quiet most of the time along the line, too; not much going on save the countermarching of troops; possibly General Grant is covering another flank movement; enemy seem to be in force on the south side of Little river.

Friday, May 27, 1864.

As I expected the army has commenced another flank movement to the left. We were ordered to hold the line until 11 o'clock then withdraw quietly and overtake the balance of the army. Goodness! I wonder if we are always to be rear guard? It's worrying, besides, we have to march so rapidly, such duty should be passed round. We crossed the North Anna about three miles below Noles Station. It has been terrible marching the roads are so blocked with army supply wagons or trains—however we have made a thirty-mile march and find ourselves near the ford at Hanover Court House. The men stood the march well for we are on the road to Richmond. Goodness! but I'm tired.

SATURDAY, May 28, 1864.

I wrote hastily yesterday, as we were ordered to move about the time I commenced; rested well last night; marched at 7 o'clock a. m.; arrived at the Pawmunky river about noon and crossed at Nelson's Ferry on a pontoon bridge without difficulty as our cavalry held the place; did not advance far south of the river before we ran into the enemy and captured two pieces of artillery; have been building breastworks this evening; are camped on Dr. Pollard's plantation, a lovely place, but much neglected owing to the war. Slight shower just at dark.

SUNDAY, May 29, 1864.

Weather quite cool and comfortable; no fighting today; only twenty miles from Richmond—Hurrah! The negroes were much frightened when they saw the Yankee army approach, but have become very much tamed in twenty-four hours; said the Johnnies told them we had horns, would cut off their arms, etc. Poor things! they were actually frightened, and showed it by their bulging eyes, looks and manner. It was comical! General Russell has gone on a reconnoissance to Hanover Court House. It's rumored that General R. E. Lee is dead, but I believe it's a fake.

MONDAY, May 30, 1864.

Very sultry with intense heat; has not rained today as usual. We were ordered to move from Dr. Pollard's in a westerly course to the right about daylight; have been changing positions all day, and yet we have been cautiously advancing on Richmond; are now within twelve miles of the Confederate capital with the rebel army in our immediate front. In order to get here we crossed Crump's Creek towards Hanover Court House. When nearing Atler's Station about noon we were ordered back to support the Second Corps which was engaging the enemy near Totopotomy Creek. We marched in a sweltering and almost exhausted condition to the Hanover turnpikewhich we had left in the morning but soon again left it cutting cross-lots through a swamp and heavy oak forest where a road was being cut for artillery, and soon went into line of battle on the left of General Birney's Division about mid-afternoon. We were ordered to charge but the order was countermanded. The lines here ran about north and south. The enemy's picket line kept up a sharp fusilade all night, as a bluff to enable its force here to withdraw in order to form another line called the Totopotomy, so as to cover several roads leading to Richmond including the Shady Grove Church road at Hantley's Corners, and the Walnut

Grove Church road as well as the Mechanicsville turnpike, etc. Our line was changed to meet the enemy's, but we made no assault. The enemy was evidently greatly worried as it kept up a heavy artillery fire and made one or two fruitless assaults. Did they but know our strength they would know better than to charge our works; but they are plucky fellows.

Tuesday, May 31, 1864.

As beautiful a morning as I ever saw; men are feeling better since they drew rations; had been without two days; heavy skirmishing in front. Our artillery shelled the enemy out of its first line of works about noon. We moved up and occupied them without difficulty; enemy has made several useless attempts to shell us but have done no harm. Our own batteries have been shelling the enemy over us, but have wounded more of our men than the enemy. The Tenth Vermont is on the skirmish line to-night. Today's experience when our batteries threw shells over us at the enemy and hurt so many of our men was the most exasperating of the campaign. Such stupidity ought to be punished, as the artillerymen could plainly see that their shells were exploding close over us and several hundred yards short of the enemy.

Wednesday, June 1, 1864.

It has been a terribly warm day. The enemy being too well posted at Totopotomy to attack, Grant concluded to move to Cold Harbor about fifteen miles away, last night. General Sheridan had taken it yesterday afternoon but being hard pressed by the enemy's Infantry he had started to leave when he was ordered by General Meade not to do so. The Sixth Corps in accordance with this plan started for that point at about 2 o'clock this morning over a narrow road leading a part of the way through swamps which are the source of the Totopotomy and Matadequin rivers, arriving at Cold Harbor which was being held by General Custer's Cavalry, at about 2 o'clock this afternoon. Characteristic of Custer when in a hot place, his band was playing Hail Columbia while his men were fighting like Trojans to hold their ground. He had had a goodly number killed and wounded who lay on the field uncared for because all his men were absolutely required for fighting in order to hold the place. Soon the dry grass and underbrush took fire and the helpless wounded were roasted to death, their charred remains being found afterwards. It was a sad sight for any one, and especially a thoughtful person.

Our line of battle consists of the Sixth and Eighteenth Corps, Major General W. F. Smith commanding the latter of about ten thousand men just from Bermuda Hundred being on the right of the line. Our Corps with its Third, First and Second Divisions in the order named from right to left was on the left of the line. The Third Division, Sixth Corps went into line about 3 o'clock p. m. just west of an old tavern at Cold Harbor Cross Roads or Old Cold

Harbor, from which tavern the place probably took its name, owing to its custom of entertaining especially at an early day when its grounds were allowed for camping purposes to travelers and they cared mostly for themselves.

Our part of the line was in an open field behind a narrow strip of woods with the enemy's breastworks just beyond about a mile more or less away in our front. We were formed by regiments four lines deep. Our regiment was on the skirmish line all night on Totopotomy Creek, but was relieved about daylight and after a hot dusty march joined our Division in the foregoing position just in season for the assault at about 6 o'clock p. m., our brigade being on the left of our Division. We were all worn out from being on the skirmish line all night followed by a rapid but all-day march, so near asleep at times en route as to frequently actually unconsciously march into scrub trees by the wayside or anything else in the line of march before awaking. It was simply impossible to keep awake as overtaxed nature had reached its limit.

We were ordered to guide left on the First Division of the Sixth Corps in the assault, but owing to some misunderstanding at first there was some delay, but our brigade soon got in motion and advanced rapidly in unbroken lines soon all alone on its right, until broken by the woods, leaving the troops on our right far in the rear, which caused us to oblique to the right when, before we were half-way through the woods and swamp which were wider in our front than to our left, our brigade had deployed so we had only one line of battle where I was with no support on my right whatever which, owing to an enfilading fire from the enemy in that direction, greatly handicapped the right of the line here. This caused quite a sharp angle in the Union line of battle at this point, and when we were afterwards drawn back a little to connect with our right it brought our line of works here closer the enemy's than at any other point. The fact is we had no support either in rear or to our right and were in a precarious situation until drawn back in continuous line of battle with the rest of the assaulting line.

It was a determined charge though, through the woods and swamp. It was my first experience as Company Commander in an assault, and it did seem queer to step in front of my men to lead them, one of if not the youngest among them. But I was on my mettle and had I known a solid shot would have cut me in part the next second, pride would have kept me up to the rack, for the Company Commanders of the Tenth Vermont did not follow but led their men in battle ever after the first one at Locust Grove and some did there. The men of Company K are splendid fighters, and I am proud of them. If there was a man who shirked I didn't see him. They followed me splendidly, have gained my respect and esteem, and I shall hate to give up the Company when the time comes to do so.

A part of our Division together with General Emery Upton's Brigade of our Corps, quite largely went over the enemy's works in the assault to-night, but could not hold them because not supported on either flank. It was a plucky fight. Our opponents were Generals Hoke, Kershaw, Pickett and Field's Divisions. General Clingman's Brigade was on the right of Hoke's Division, and was badly broken up in the assault, as well as the Brigade on either side of his, one of which belonged to Kershaw's Division. Our regiment captured the Fifty-first North Carolina Infantry, the commanding officer of which surrendered his sword to Captain E. B. Frost of Company A, acting Major. Our Division and Upton's Brigade captured five hundred prisoners, most of whom were probably taken by our regiment. Such as were taken by it were sent to the rear, without guard, but were again picked up en route so we got no credit for them. We could not spare men to send them under guard for we had more than we could do to hold the works after taking them.

The loss in the Sixth Corps was twelve hundred, of which over eight hundred were from our Division. The splendid work of the Third Division here put it in full fellowship with the rest of the Sixth Corps. We had proved our mettle grandly even if a shorter time in service than the Second and Third Divisions. The loss from our Brigade was twenty-one officers, seven of whom were killed, ten wounded and four were taken prisoners; one hundred enlisted men were also killed and two hundred and seventy-five wounded. Our regiment lost nineteen killed and sixty-two wounded, and Company K, one killed and four wounded. Lieutenant Colonel Townsend of the One Hundred and Sixth New York, Lieutenants Ezra Stetson of Company B, and C. G. Newton of Company G, Tenth Vermont, were killed; Colonel W. W. Henry and Lieutenant William White of the Tenth Vermont, Colonel W. S. Truex of the Fourteenth New Jersey, commanding First Brigade, Colonel Schall of the Eighty-seventh Pennsylvania were wounded, and Major McDonald of the One Hundred and Sixth New York and Lieutenant J. S. Thompson of Company A, Tenth Vermont were taken prisoners and two other officers.

THURSDAY, June 2, 1864.

Oh, dear, another shocking battle on hand! But we can lick them! I dread it, though! We laid on our arms in line of battle last night; heavy skirmishing continued in our front all night; built rifle pits this morning; men very tired; ordered to assault this evening at 4 o'clock, but it rained and the order was countermanded until morning thus prolonging the agony; drew rations for the Company to-night; am getting very tired of this campaign and shall be glad when it's over, but I suppose it will last a month longer. The enemy is doing its utmost to gain a victory, but God grant that we may be the victors if it is His will.

FRIDAY, June 3, 1864.

It still continues to rain a little, but for all this the Second, Sixth and Eighteenth Corps in the order mentioned from right to left, were ordered to charge at 4 o'clock a. m. and not to fire a shot until we got on to the enemy's works, but the charge was not a success. We never even reached the enemy's works. The attack commenced on the right and ran along the line until it reached the left. We advanced under a murderous fire in our front from the enemy's artillery, sharpshooters and when in range of its main line of battle and were simply slaughtered. We have lost to-day over 4,000 in killed and wounded. The total casualties June first and third have been 12,000, of which about 10,000 have been killed and wounded. The number killed in the Tenth Vermont since Tuesday is twenty-two and one hundred and twenty-nine wounded; and in Company K to-day one killed and five wounded. Two killed and nine wounded in two days greatly weakens my command. Captains Lucius T. Hunt and Pearl D. Blodgett were wounded, and Captain E. B. Frost was shot through the head and killed after the assault, by a sharpshooter. The Tenth Vermont lost sixty-two to-day in killed and wounded. We are now intrenching and ordered to act on the defensive. The men of Company K are cool, splendid fighters.

As I sat on the ground this morning with my back against a sapling in the woods, a sharpshooter planked a bullet in the ground about an inch from the calf of my right leg which covered me with flying dirt. He could see my blue pants through the green foliage. I moved. Colonel Schall who was wounded in the arm in the assault on June first and carried it in a sling in the fight to-day, was again wounded in the same arm. He is not a man to take advantage of a wound not totally disabling him to get out of a fight, evidently.

SATURDAY, June 4, 1864.

The enemy made two unsuccessful assaults last night. Reinforcements are arriving rapidly. The rain yesterday and this afternoon has greatly cooled the air. There has been considerable cannonading on both sides and heavy skirmishing all day. The lines of battle in our immediate front are only about eight hundred yards apart and the skirmish lines are very near each other. The One Hundred and Sixth New York Volunteer Infantry, our favorite fighting companion as a regiment, are digging another line of rifle pits in our front for the pickets. I got a letter from Captain H. R. Steele this afternoon. General Grant issued an order to-day for the army to act on the defensive. Good!

SUNDAY, June 5, 1864.

It rained nearly all the forenoon, but the skirmishers didn't seem to mind it, but kept on fighting. It was cloudy and sultry all this afternoon, but there was no rain. The enemy tried to assault about dark last night, but gave it up as our artillery had an enfilading fire on them. There was a very heavy rolling musketry fire on our distant right about midnight, but I don't know the reason of it. The enemy tried to carry our left flank about dark by storm, but failed. The roll of artillery and musketry fire was appalling for about a half hour, and the slaughter must have been great. Golly! this is stubborn fighting again! I'm proud of both armies. I wonder what the Johnnies think of us as fighters now? I'm sure they fight hard enough for me.

Monday, June 6, 1864.

To-day has been sweltering hot. We lay in our works until about dark when a part of our regiment was ordered for picket. I am not detailed this time. Lieutenants Merritt Barber and George E. Davis, Tenth Vermont, reported for duty this afternoon. Lieutenant-Colonel W. W. Henry's commission as Colonel Tenth Vermont came, also Major C. G. Chandler's as Lieutenant-Colonel. Captain Samuel Darrah was shot through the head this afternoon by a sharpshooter while sitting by his Company, and died at 2 o'clock p. m. His remains will be sent to Vermont. He was my captain and I am very sorry for his untimely end. He was a brave little fellow, jolly, clever and kind, always full of life and will be greatly missed. A flag of truce was sent out in front of our division to-day; don't know what it was for; has been quiet all day; men all burrowed under bomb-proof covers. We sunk big square holes in the ground about two feet deep large enough to hold about eight or more men, and roofed them with logs, brush and dirt, but it's very warm to have to live so. It's fine, though, when bombs are bursting which they often do.

Tuesday, June 7, 1864.

It has been very quiet along the lines all day; both sides seem to be tired of sharpshooting. Another flag of truce was sent out to-day, I think to get permission to bury our dead between the lines of which there are *many* plainly to be seen and they are commencing to smell bad; am told Major Crandall of the Sixth Vermont, just to the right of us, was shot to-day by a sharpshooter. He was a popular student once at Barre Academy, Vermont. Captain Edwin Dillingham reported for duty to-day; has been prisoner of war at Richmond since the battle of Locust Grove, Va. last fall; never saw him looking better; is a handsome man, anyway, and a gentleman. Our army seems to be lying idle now, except the heavy artillery which is building forts in our rear; occasionally hear the report of siege guns to our left—or we suppose them to be siege guns.

Wednesday, June 8, 1864.

Still we remain in the same position. Both armies seem to be preparing for defense operations. I have no doubt but what Grant intends to hold this line, but I think it far from his intentions to attack the rebs here again. Probably he will soon move round Lee's left flank and then perhaps build another chain of forts; really hope he will manage in some way to get round so much assaulting; enemy threw a few shells just at dark which all went over us; no change to-night.

Thursday, June 9, 1864.

Very warm all day; sharpshooters keep pecking away at us but don't accomplish much. Occasionally a shell has been thrown by each side all day; enemy seems to throw shells oftener at night; shall be glad when we are out of range of the enemy's sharpshooters for one. It's not comfortable to be shot at every time one shows himself in daylight; have been writing letters to-day, one to Pert and another to Susan Wheeler; enemy shelling quite lively to-night, but shells all go over us and explode far in our rear among the camp-followers and hospitals where it is said to be more dangerous than here at the front, they suffer greatly from shells there.

Friday, June 10, 1864.

Oh, dear! Another day finds us in the same old position. I wonder if this awful war will ever find an end? It looks worse to me than ever. Here we are within ten miles of Richmond, and I can't see any prospect of our ever getting nearer to it without sacrificing half our noble army, and this in my opinion won't pay. But I fear I am getting faint-hearted! I must have more faith in our Generals. Indeed, I think I have faith in them, but they can't do what they want without they have the men to do it with.

Saturday, June 11, 1864.

Goodness! We traveled all night and haven't got out of sight of our old position. Did ever anyone see such stupidity? I'm getting more fault-finding than an old maid, but loss of sleep and shattered nerves from being overtaxed in every way will account for it. Nature will collapse when continually overtaxed. I'm all out of patience, but it will do no good to mutter, so I'll stop. We relieved a portion of the Second Corps to-day; don't know where they are going; probably some strategic movement afoot; was sent out on picket about noon. It's not a very agreeable job to relieve the skirmish line in daylight when the enemy is so near, yet we did it; heavy cannonading to-night.

Sunday, June 12, 1864.

Relieved the skirmish line yesterday without great difficulty; all quiet through the night; not a gun fired to-day thus far in front of us; can hear the rebs talk and sing quite plain in our immediate front; was informed this afternoon the army would move to-night at 7 o'clock; dread leaving the skirmish line, but I suppose we can do it; very quiet this evening; bands playing and big guns booming; wonder if it isn't a bluff? The moon is shining brightly.

Monday, June 13, 1864.

The effective force of our regiment now is twelve officers and three hundred and fifty-two enlisted men. We left Vermont with a thousand enlisted men or more. I wrote hastily last evening, being crowded for time. I left the skirmish line in the dark without difficulty, but it was very nerve-trying. My post was in second growth hard timber, and the enemy could be plainly heard creeping up close—very close, within a few feet, to see if we had gone after dark. When one's alone in the dark under such circumstances and he don't know but what all his comrades are miles away on the march except his part of the skirmish line, such conditions are disconcerting, for pickets are sometimes sacrificed when an army moves. The enemy mistrusting our designs followed us up closely—so close we had to run with hair on end to get away without drawing their fire for if we did it meant perhaps that we would be abandoned to our fate by the assembled picket a goodly distance off awaiting us. But O, what a relief it was when we joined the reserve! We were on the extreme left and the last to leave the enemy's front as our position protected our army in its flank movement. It was the most trying similar position I have ever been in up to this time during the war. We traveled like racehorses all night and to-day, and I, at least, was frequently so near asleep while marching in the heat of the day, as to unconsciously walk right up against any object in my path which would of course arouse me; marched about twenty miles, but I should think it was forty—indeed, forty is what we called it at the time—via Charles City Court House and bivouaced at Jones bridge on the Chickahominy. I don't think I was ever so tired in my life as to-night; don't think I *could* march much further; got a daily paper to-day for the first time since we left our winter quarters. We were the rear of the army last night, and it was a trial to wait after leaving the skirmish line till all the men of the Division assembled before taking up our line of march. I got testy several times in the night walking into scrub trees by the wayside half asleep. We laughed at each other for doing it, though, for we have our fun even under the most trying circumstances.

Tuesday, June 14, 1864.

Very cool and comfortable for this season; marched about six miles this morning and went into camp; have remained here all day and possibly shall tonight; hope to at any rate for I am very tired and need rest; was ordered back to take command of Company D this morning; am not much sorry for the change for it's my Company. We are only a short distance from the James river; can hear the steamboats whistle plainly. It does seem *so* good not to hear musketry and picket firing, but from force of habit I hear both in my sleep nights. Our army excepting the First and Third Divisions of our Corps crossed the river here to-day on a pontoon bridge. It took one hundred pontoons to construct the bridge which is held in place by large vessels at anchor above and below the bridge, especially during the ebb and flow of the tide which is about four feet. For the last ten miles before reaching here we passed through a fine country and community with fine old plantations and houses surrounded with lovely flowers and beautifully embowered.

WEDNESDAY, June 15, 1864.

Weather quite warm all day; about 9 o'clock a. m. changed positions to the left; remained till night, and then moved still further to the left and finally camped for the night. A part of the regiment has gone on picket. I am not going; no news to-day. I have been thinking quite seriously that I will go home this winter and fit myself for a profession—not that I am getting tired of military life but think it for my interests in the long run; am undecided what I will do. I don't believe I shall be a quitter, though, for I am not weak that way. No patriot resigns in the face of the enemy when his country needs his services.

THURSDAY, June 16, 1864.

About 5 o'clock a. m. a small force including our regiment, moved down within about three quarters of a mile of the James river, formed line of battle and threw up rifle pits; remained here until about 4 o'clock p. m. when we were relieved by General Burnside's Division of colored troops. We then marched down to the river and took transports for Point of Rocks; the Tenth Vermont was favored by going on the dispatch boat; had plenty of room and a fine time. The quiet moonlight night and cool river breeze were delightfully enchanting after such war experiences as we had passed through. It seemed heavenly! I withdrew to a lonely corner by myself and gave myself up to reflection and feelings of thankfulness; has been hot all day. It is reported that General W. F. Smith has taken the outer works of Petersburg, Va., captured sixteen pieces of artillery and twenty-five hundred prisoners. I hardly believe it. I know what such fighting means too well. Such victories don't grow on bushes to be plucked by every one passing.

FRIDAY, June 17, 1864.

We arrived at Point of Rocks at 1 o'clock a. m., marched about three miles, got coffee and joined our brigade in General B. F. Butler's breastworks at the front; have been idle all day. About dark our skirmish line was driven in, and our regiment was sent out to support the line until reestablished, but as they could not succeed in this we withdrew and went back to camp. We expected to have to assault the enemy's formidable fortifications, and were greatly relieved when we were withdrawn. General H. G. Wright opposed General Butler in an assault on the enemy's works here and won his point, it is said.

S<small>ATURDAY</small>, June 18, 1864.

The number of prisoners captured yesterday by General Smith was only about five hundred, not twenty-five hundred as reported. The works were carried by storm by colored troops, but they couldn't have taken them if the forts had been fully garrisoned, by veterans instead of citizens. We have remained behind our works all day; brisk skirmishing in front, and cannonading towards Petersburg; gunboats have thrown a few shells into the enemy's lines. I got letters from home to-night; all well there.

S<small>UNDAY</small>, June 19, 1864.

It was warm and sultry in the middle of the day. We remained in our works till about 5 o'clock p. m. when on being relieved by General W. F. Smith's command, we at once started for Petersburg about eight miles away to rejoin the Army of the Potomac, crossing the Appomattox river on the pontoon bridge, and arriving at the outer works about 8 o'clock p. m. where we bivouaced. Generals Grant and Butler rode along the lines together at Bermuda Hundred this afternoon. It was my first sight of Butler; queer-looking man; his beauty won't kill him.

M<small>ONDAY</small>, June 20, 1864.

Have just returned from the heights. The City of Petersburg looks lovely at a distance, but our guns command it and can at any time lay it in ruins. The enemy occupy the heights on the other side of the Appomattox river. Siege guns are shelling back and forth, but it's no such fighting as we have seen since we broke winter quarters. We have remained in the woods all day, it's been so warm. Orry Blanchard called to-night; am detailed for fatigue—probably to work a detail on fortifications.

T<small>UESDAY</small>, June 21, 1864.

I worked a fatigue party on a fort all night arriving in camp about 5 o'clock a. m. tired and hungry; slept until about 6 o'clock p. m. when we were ordered to march. We moved out on the Jerusalem plank road to where our cavalry were skirmishing on the ground to the left of our army which we were expected to occupy, and halted about 9 o'clock p. m. Although it was dark we threw out a skirmish line, forced the enemy back, captured several prisoners, camped and commenced to throw up breastworks having joined our line with the Second Corps on our right. The First, Second and Third Divisions, Sixth Corps, in the order mentioned from the right now form the left of our army. General Grant is simply extending his line to the left. Colonel W. W. Henry took command of the regiment last night. I have received a letter from Lieutenant G. E. Davis at Annapolis; is doing well. The One Hundred and Sixth New York captured a Johnny to-night under singular circumstances but I've not room to relate them.

WEDNESDAY, June 22, 1864.

It's very warm and dry and the dust is intolerable it's so sandy. We remained in our rifle pits until about 9 o'clock a. m. when we advanced and finding the enemy gone occupied their works till about 3 o'clock p. m. when we threw up another line of pits, and were then ordered to fall back to our line of last night, but finally charged through the brush about two miles and captured another line of works without resistance. There has been considerable confusion to-day. While on the skirmish line the Eighty-seventh Pennsylvania of our brigade came near being captured from the fact that for some unaccountable reason the picket line next on one of its flanks was withdrawn unknown to Colonel Schall, when the enemy crept through the opening and captured about a dozen men, but seeing what was the matter, Colonel Schall, a splendid officer, took such action as was necessary and saved his regiment. In another instance the First Division of our Corps, which had moved more slowly than ours and not as wished, found itself and its skirmish line partly a goodly distance behind our division. It was amusing to say the least, at any rate to us. We finally got things straightened out with the Second Division on our left but considerably in rear with its left refused to protect its flank. The first Division occupied a similar position on our right but a goodly distance in our rear.

THURSDAY, June 23, 1864.

This has been the warmest day yet this summer, and no sign of rain. We remained in line all day without intrenching when the enemy began to make quite a demonstration on our left. We threw up rifle pits but our division was so far in advance of the other two of our Corps, the rebs had a cross fire on us. Our skirmishers have been on the Weldon railroad most of the day until finally the First Division of our Corps began to destroy the track. It had only just begun when the force sent from the Vermont Brigade and the Eighty-seventh Pennsylvania of our brigade to protect it, were attacked, surrounded and about five hundred, including four officers and seventy-nine enlisted men from the Eighty-seventh, were either killed or taken prisoners. The Eighty-seventh had twenty-six killed and wounded. After this we all retired to the line occupied by us on the 21st of June.

FRIDAY, June 24, 1864.

Intensely warm and still; no prospect of rain; remained in our rear line of works until about 9 o'clock a. m. when we received orders to move out by the left flank into our first line of works. Our skirmish line has been driven in once and probably five hundred were taken prisoners by the enemy. This is rather discouraging but we must expect to meet with some reverses. Rebel prisoners have been sent in to-day; they speak hopefully of their cause, but I have *no* doubt but what the *Union* cause will triumph.

Saturday, June 25, 1864.

Still we are behind our works sweltering in the sun. The only way we can possibly keep comfortable is to stick up brush which gives us a little shade; enemy made no attack last night as expected on our left. The Second Corps was attacked during the night, the enemy gaining some advantage, but our troops rallied and regained what they had lost. It's quite comfortable this evening; the bands are all playing, and seem determined to help us pass the time as pleasantly as possible in spite of our uncomfortable surroundings. But if we are uncomfortable what condition must the enemy be in? It's a poor soldier who never thinks of such things.

Sunday, June 26, 1864.

Another Sabbath morning has dawned, and finds us in the same uncomfortable position as yesterday, yet I will not complain of the intense heat as long as we can remain quiet. We get plenty of lemons and ice from the Sanitary Commission which alleviates our discomforts considerably. The enemy still permits us to remain quiet, but are less lenient to those on our right, as fighting was kept up all night. Burnside was attacked but held his own.

Monday, June 27, 1864.

There was considerable thunder during the night, but no rain here, yet it has been cooler to-day than yesterday. We have a few lemons left. Captain Edwin Dillingham's commission as Major came this forenoon; regiment goes on picket to-night; slight shower with thunder about 4 o'clock p. m. and it's cooler.

Tuesday, June 28, 1864.

We relieved the Fourteenth New Jersey from picket; all quiet through the night; made my headquarters with the reserve in an orchard where we got plenty of green apples, etc.; was relieved by the One Hundred and Sixth New York after dark. On returning from picket was happily surprised to find that preparations had been made to go into camp, and that the men of my Company had a tent all up for me. The Company (D) generally looks after me very nicely. This Company, too, is a splendid fighting one with me, anyway; but, as we have been in tight places, I guess K Company has won my admiration as a valiant one over all others, except Company B, which will follow me anywhere I lead, as it did over the fence at Locust Grove, Va. in a plucky charge for which we never got credit. It was only bandbox soldiers who were seen that day and mentioned in orders.

Wednesday, June 29, 1864.

Very warm and dry again this morning. General H. G. Wright, our corps commander, had an inspection and review at 7 o'clock this morning. It seemed so strange to be called out again for parade I hardly knew how to act. But what seems strange is that they should commence this thing when the men are all tired out. They need a day's rest more than anything else. I do wish they would consider the welfare of the men more. Well, here we are again! have marched all afternoon and turned up at Reames Station on the Weldon railroad; didn't know but what we were marching round to go into the back door of Petersburg or Richmond. I'm half dead with fatigue.

Thursday, June 30, 1864.

Quite warm, but a fairly cool breeze. The First and Second Divisions of our Corps worked all night destroying the railroad and are at it now, our forces having burnt the depot; have made thorough work of it; think it must have been quite a business place here once, but it is now a mass of ruins. Our division has been building breastworks; had just got them nicely completed when we were ordered back late in the day to our old position as we supposed, but 9 o'clock p. m. finds us in camp for the night two miles from there.

Friday, July 1, 1864.

Well, here it is the first day of July! Who would think it? We have been fighting two months, and the time (July 4th), set by thousands for the downfall of the Confederate capital is close at hand, yet it cannot be taken by that time. Still I have no doubt there are thousands at the North who are expecting to hear of its capture, and perhaps many who are foolish enough to believe that it will surely fall on July 4th. I have no doubt but what it will fall before another summer, but it will take time and hard fighting, and many a poor fellow on both sides will bite the dust first; wonder if all think of this? Many never think of anything till it happens, they are tooselfish; remained all day in the position we took up last night, but just at night we moved a quarter of a mile to the front and formed line of battle.

Saturday, July 2, 1864.

This morning we started about 7 o'clock for camp and arrived about 10 o'clock a. m.; have had directions to fix up quarters as there is a prospect of remaining in camp several days; are obeying orders of course, but I suspect we shall move before three days; very warm day—sweltering.

Sunday, July 3, 1864.

We have made arrangements so that we are quite comfortable in spite of the intense heat; has been very quiet in camp all day. All are anticipating a good time to-morrow if General Grant don't conclude to have us fight, and I don't think he will, for I don't believe he considers it of any use to attack the enemy, so long as he can oblige it to come out and fight him. Lieutenant G. E. Davis came to-day. Lieutenant H. W. Kingsley called to-night.

MONDAY, July 4, 1864.

Again another Fourth of July has come and, not as usual for the past three years, all is quiet. Who could have anticipated it with such conditions? It's very warm and dusty. Lieutenant Hill and I have been down to the Division hospital to see Lieutenant H. W. Kingsley. It has been the quietest time in camp to-day we have had in two months; have enjoyed it greatly. Colonel Henry Powell—a good soldier—formerly First Sergeant of Company F, Tenth Vermont, but promoted Colonel of U. S. C. T.called to-day. I don't think he has a very exalted opinion of colored troops and he may be right; he's a man of good sense and judgment.

TUESDAY, July 5, 1864.

Quite comfortable all day. Lieut. G. E. Davis has completed the Muster and Pay rolls, but I've not felt very well and have been abed all day. Captain G. W. Burnell, formerly Second Lieutenant, Tenth Vermont, has been with us to-day; he's about the same old chap, but I don't think he has a very high opinion of colored troops, either. It's reported the enemy is making a raid into Maryland with General Jubal A. Early in command. I have been expecting this. They will doubtless make us much trouble, but they can't checkmate Grant in that way; he has too many men. He won't budge from here—*never*—until he takes Petersburg which means Richmond, too. Up to this time our First Brigade has lost in killed, wounded, etc., over eight hundred men since we broke winter camp.

WEDNESDAY, July 6, 1864.

Our Division was ordered to move to City Point at daylight to take transports for Baltimore, Md., and thence by rail to Harper's Ferry, Md., or vicinity. I said we'd move shortly when ordered to fix camp on the second of July. We arrived at City Point about 3 o'clock p. m. after a hot dusty march and much suffering, and sailed about 4 o'clock p. m. It's quick work to load a boat in an hour, but Grant was there. The contrast from marching through sand ankle deep as dry as an ash heap with the air so thick with dust one a few steps away is invisible, and being on the cool river is a great transformation we much appreciate— Hallelujah!

THURSDAY, July 7, 1864.

I was told last night that we should reach Fortress Monroe at daylight, and I was up to see it, but we passed it about midnight. We are evidently greatly needed to head off a raid in Maryland. I saw the sun rise on the water this morning. It has been quite warm all day although on the water with the boat making good time. We arrived at Baltimore at 4 o'clock p. m. but have not been allowed to leave the boat yet.

FRIDAY, July 8, 1864.

Two boat-loads of our Division landed last night at 11 o'clock. We took the cars at once for Frederick, Md., and arrived there at 10 o'clock a. m. to-day, finding the city nearly deserted by its inhabitants, and only a small force of hundred days' men, etc., to defend it having skirmished yesterday with the enemy's advanced guard and kept it from entering the town. The place is full of rumors, but it's impossible to get any reliable information. We were followed this afternoon by more of our Division, and all have been kept busy by General Lew Wallace who is in command, marching about the city, forming lines of battle to the north of it, etc., presumably to try and deceive the enemy as to our strength.

There were in Frederick on our arrival here together with such troops as have arrived since, not including our Division, twenty-five hundred green troops under Brigadier-General E. B. Tyler, which have never been under fire to any extent, as follows: Five companies of the First Regiment Maryland Home Brigade, Captain Chas. J. Brown commanding; the Third Regiment Maryland Home Brigade, Colonel Chas. Gilpin commanding; the Eleventh Regiment Maryland Infantry, Colonel Wm. T. Landstreet commanding; three companies of the One Hundred and Forty-fourth Regiment Ohio National Guard, Colonel Allison L. Brown commanding; seven companies of the One Hundred and Forty-ninth Regiment Ohio National Guard, Colonel A. L. Brown commanding; and Captain F. W. Alexander's Baltimore (Md.) Battery of six three-inch guns; Lieut. Colonel David R. Clendenin's squadron of Mounted Infantry from the Eighth Illinois National Guard; a detachment of mounted infantry—probably two companies—from the One Hundred and Fifty-ninth Ohio National Guard, Captains E. H. Lieb and H. S. Allen commanding, respectively; the Loudoun (Va.) Rangers, and a detachment of mixed cavalry, Major Charles A. Wells commanding. The Eleventh Maryland and all the Ohio troops are hundred days' men.

The Third Division, Major General James B. Ricketts commanding, of the Sixth Corps, consists of two brigades and now has here nine of its twelve regiments or a force of three thousand three hundred and fifty men as follows: The First Brigade is commanded by Colonel W. S. Truex of the Fourteenth Regiment New Jersey Infantry, and is composed of the One Hundred and

Sixth Regiment New York Volunteer Infantry, Captain E. M. Paine commanding; the Tenth Regiment Vermont Volunteer Infantry, Colonel W. W. Henry commanding; the One Hundred and Fifty-first Regiment New York Volunteer Infantry, Colonel William Emerson commanding; the Eighty-seventh Regiment Pennsylvania Volunteer Infantry, Lieutenant-Colonel J. A. Stahel commanding, and the Fourteenth Regiment New Jersey Infantry, Lieutenant-Colonel C. K. Hall commanding. The Second Brigade, Colonel Matthews R. McClennan commanding is composed of the Ninth Regiment New York Heavy Artillery, Colonel Wm. H. Seward, Jr. commanding; the One Hundred and Twenty-sixth Regiment Ohio National Guard, Lieutenant-Colonel Aaron W. Ebright commanding; the One Hundred and Tenth Regiment Ohio National Guard, Lieutenant-Colonel Otho H. Binkley commanding; the One Hundred and Thirty-eighth Regiment Pennsylvania Infantry, Major Lewis A. May commanding; and a detachment of the One Hundred and Twenty-second Ohio Infantry commanded by Lieutenant C. J. Gibson. The Sixth Regiment Maryland Infantry, Sixty-second Regiment Pennsylvania Infantry and most of the One Hundred and Twenty-second Regiment of Ohio National Guard of the Second Brigade have not yet arrived.

With the Georgetown or Washington and Baltimore turnpikes both passing through Frederick, it is easy to see why this is an important point as viewed from a military standpoint. The latter runs in a westerly direction from Baltimore, crosses the Monocacy river over a stone bridge about three miles from, and on through, Frederick centrally, and thence on to Harper's Ferry, Frederick being about thirty-five miles from Baltimore. The Georgetown turnpike runs northwesterly crossing the Monocacy river on a covered wooden bridge at Frederick Junction, about three miles from Frederick, on through the city which is also about thirty-five miles from Washington, and thence northwesterly to Sharpsburg, the two pikes crossing each other centrally in Frederick at right angles. The Georgetown wooden and railroad steel bridges across the Monocacy at Frederick Junction are about one-fourth of a mile apart, and the distance between the Georgetown pike wooden bridge and Baltimore turnpike stone bridge is about three miles with Crum's Ford about midway between. There are also several fords within two miles or so below theGeorgetown pike wooden bridge where it crosses the Monocacy at Frederick Junction.

SATURDAY, July 9, 1864.

We left Frederick under the cover of darkness last night, and after marching a round-about way which took nearly all night, brought up at Frederick Junction, about three miles away on the Baltimore and Ohio railroad, where on a ridge of hills skirting the Monocacy river probably on an average eighty feet high more or less across and on the east side of the river opposite the junction the railroad steel and Georgetown turnpike covered wooden bridges, the latter of which we burnt early in the day to keep the enemy from crossing—we formed line of battle in a naturally strong position about 7 o'clock a. m. probably about three miles long. The river was virtually crescent-shaped opposite the Third Division with the concave side towards Frederick, but a little way above the railroad bridge ran northwesterly for fully six miles or more, it being about three miles distant from the Baltimore pike stone bridge northeasterly from Frederick, and the same distance southeasterly to the Georgetown pike wooden bridge. A skirmish line of two hundred and seventy-five enlisted men and three officers was established as soon as practicable under the command of Maj. C. G. Chandler. It was also crescent-shaped with the convex side also towards Frederick with its flanks resting practically on the river. Captain C. J. Brown and two hundred enlisted men were from General E. B. Tyler's command, and Major C. G. Chandler, First Lieut. G. E. Davis and seventy-five enlisted men were from General J. B. Rickett's Third Division of the Sixth Corps, the latter officers,—Davis and Chandler,—being from the Tenth Vermont. Here we waited for the enemy to approach. We didn't have long to wait for soon the whole country across the Monocacy was alive with Johnnies who attacked us with overwhelming numbers about 8 o'clock a. m. and kept it up till about 5 o'clock p. m.

It was a brilliant little fight on our part, although when we formed line we were much depressed for we knew we were greatly outnumbered. General E. B. Tyler guarded the Baltimore pike stone bridge with a goodly portion of his command, and Crum's Ford with three companies of Colonel Gilpin's regiment of the Potomac Home Brigade. At first three pieces of Captain Alexander's Battery were given General Ricketts who protected the railroad bridge and Georgetown pike, and three pieces were given General Tyler but later only one piece. The left of our main line was refused or bent back just north of the Thomas house, Colonel Clendenin's squadron of cavalry being far to our left. Our infantry left ran along the Georgetown turnpike which led to the wooden bridge burnt early in the morning to keep the enemy from crossing. The pike runs as a whole from the river about southeast forming an obtuse angle with it, and it was along it which runs through a slight cut here, which formed an excellent natural breastwork, Company D of Burlington, Vt., and two other companies of the Tenth Vermont were stretched out fully a quarter of a mile or more under Major E. Dillingham of our regiment his right being near the junction of the Georgetown pike and the Urbana road. It was little more than an attenuated skirmish line but nevertheless the main line of battle. The command of Company D fell to me as Lieut. G. E. Davis was on the skirmish line. It was an anxious time for having little faith in our cavalry I feared a cavalry charge from the enemy down the pike to my left, as a sharp cavalry skirmish had occurred here when this part of the field had been first occupied by our forces in the morning before my arrival. The skirmishers in my front were very busy, too, exchanging shots with the enemy's skirmishers till the first assault by the enemy in the afternoon about 2 o'clock on the east side of the river which was a brilliant one. The enemy in strong force had forded the river a goodly distance south of us, left its horses out of sight and appeared from the edge of the woods on top of a high hill bordering the river about three-quarters of a mile away to the south in solid lines which moved in double time down the long green sloping open field in perfect order all the while shouting their ominous defiant battle cry. It was General McCausland's Brigade of dismounted cavalry in two lines; and let me say right here that if this was an average sized brigade in Early's army then half the truth as to its numbers has not been told. I could see this assaulting column being nearest to it probably, better than any other officer on the field, and *know* whereof I write.

The long swaying lines of grey in perfect cadence with glistening guns and brasses, and above all the proudly borne but to us hated banner of the Confederacy with its stars and bars, was a spectacle rarely surpassed in the bright sunlight of a perfect summer day. I for one looked on the scene with mingled feelings of bitterness, dread and awe, for they were so far away there was nothing else to do. As soon as they first appeared on the hill all firing largely ceased in my front on the skirmish lines and everything was as hushed later save the indistinct distant battle cry of the enemy as on a Sabbath day even the men looking at the spectacle in silent awe for apparently the enemy which greatly outnumbered us, was making directly for our part of the line. On, on, they came down the long slope, through a wide little valley out of sight every moment seeming an age until finally they appeared about a half mile away still in excellent order when they slightly changed direction to their left along the hills near the river which greatly relieved my anxiety inasmuch as we wouldn't have to bear the brunt of the attack; but a suspicion of being cut off from the rest of the line and captured, which I feared a little later, made the situation still more trying. On they came, swaying first one way and then another, keeping us in breathless suspense, but determined to hold our ground as long as possible when the shock of battle should come. Finally as they got near enough to be shelled our artillery opened on them to our right and then the infantry supporting it when the enemy's lines wavered and broke and they were temporarily repulsed until reinforced. I was then ordered with Company D about a half mile more or less to my right nearer the left centre of our line from the railroad to support with others four or more guns of Alexander's battery, in a sharp artillery duel with the enemy across the Monocacy in which First Lieutenant C. E. Evans, an unassuming, quiet officer, but good fighter, took an active part and did excellent work, together with Second Lieutenant P. Leary—now Brigadier-General U. S. A., retired—of that battery. It was here, too, that I was painfully wounded by an exploding shell from the enemy on the tip of the right hip bone. It was so bad that Major J. A. Salsbury of my regiment advised me to go to Colonel Henry for permission to go to the rear as it was well known that soon the Union forces would have to hastily retreat as the enemy had crossed the Monocacy river on both flanks and were fast surrounding our intrepid little force with overwhelming numbers, which, when the order came to retreat meant a rapid one and Salsbury, an elderly man, did not think me in condition to keep from being captured.

Knowing that every one who possibly could should remain on the fighting line in such a vital emergency as the possible loss of the National Capital, and especially an officer, for the effect such an example would have on the men, and being the only officer with and in command of my Company, I declined to ask for such permission. Major Salsbury rather emphatically in effect replied: "If you don't go and ask Colonel Henry for permission to go to the rear, I shall go myself!" and he did. Before he returned, the whole limb having been numbed by the shock produced by the shell, the reaction had caused excruciating pain, especially at the sensitive point where the glancing butt end of a shell in full flight had mangled the flesh and turned it black and blue for several inches around. It was the sensitive end of the hip bone, however, which afterwards affected the whole limb producing with age numbness especially in the toes and heel of the foot and of the whole limb when on horseback scouting for Indians after the Civil War, which disability was one of the principal causes of my retirement from active service in the regular army in 1885, that was most affected. Lying on the ground with blanched face and clenched teeth to keep from crying out with pain, which pride prevented, Major Salsbury returned, and to my amusement, even in such circumstances, jerkily took the position of a soldier, saluted his junior officer, then a Second Lieutenant, who was still lying on the ground in great distress, in the most respectful and dignified way saying, disappointedly, sympathetically and snappishly, for obvious reasons, with an anxious look: "Colonel Henry has denied my request!" or to that effect.

While these events were transpiring, First Lieutenant G. E. Davis, of Company D, Tenth Vermont, who after Captain Samuel Darrah of that Company—a most intrepid fighter,—was killed at Cold Harbor, had commanded Company D, but was now in command of the skirmish line on the opposite or west side of the Monocacy River where he so ably directed, fought and finally withdrew it with so much dash,—he and some of his men sensationally escaping by running along the ties under fire across the open railroad bridge forty feet above the water, Private Thomas O'Brien of Company D, Tenth Vermont, falling through the bridge into the river and escaping,—as to attract the attention of General Lew Wallace, and thereby won lasting fame and was also awarded a Medal of Honor later on. For some reason Major C. G. Chandler had left his command, when it fell to Captain C. J. Brown, the next in rank, who, being inexperienced, and the skirmishers in a hot place and hard pressed, sensibly relinquished his command to Lieutenant Davis who had had more experience, and thus had enviable fame and valor most dramatically forced upon him, although he was grandly equal to the emergency.

Within a very short time after I was wounded the valiant little command was in places virtually cutting its way through the enemy's lines, which almost completely enveloped it, in full retreat. It was during this time that one of the color guard, Corporal Alexander Scott, a brave and efficient soldier of the same Company (D, of Burlington), who was retreating near me under a hot fusilade of shot and shell, saved the regimental colors from capture for which he deservedly afterwards, partly on my recommendation, received a Medal of Honor. But I did not take to being captured as some who were even able-bodied did, and hobbled away. Feeling piqued, however, because not allowed to go sooner to the rear from the battlefield in my maimed condition—although I would not have gone anyway, but wanted permission because I thought I deserved it, as up to that time I had never asked to do so in any battle—still I made no complaint to anyone afterwards, but stubbornly, grieved and in constant pain, marched with my command all night and the following day to the Relay House, near Baltimore, bathing the wound occasionally en route with cool water from a friendly well or running stream as I passed, which was a great relief. But my feelings were greatly wounded at the lack of consideration received, as I thought, from Colonel Henry. As my pride got the best of my judgment I have suffered in consequence ever since. Had I ridden instead of marched, it would have at least saved a game leg and hip of undue strain and possibly from disappointing results afterwards, for had I been in active service at the breaking out of the Spanish-American war, as I would have been but for this wound, it goes without saying that I would then have been given high rank with others of my rank at that time and in the end retired from active service with the rank any way of Major-General.

Owing to a greatly superior force we were obliged to fall back in disorder having eleven officers and five hundred and forty enlisted men captured and leaving most of our wounded and dead on the field.

For some unaccountable reason the three regiments of the Second Brigade mentioned in this diary yesterday as not having arrived were detained at Monrovia, Md., a station on the Baltimore and Ohio railroad about eight miles east of Monocacy and were not in the fight. If they had been, I believe we could have stood the enemy off even longer than we did, and Early might not think of appearing before Washington—though this is doubtful—which he may now do. I cannot understand though, why veteran troops should have been kept in reserve if such was the case in such a contingency—the capital of the nation being in jeopardy—instead of hundred days' men or in fact any force whatever. It seems to me that in case they were not kept in reserve purposely by competent authority, someone should be courtmartialed and punished, let it fall where it may, and that General Lew Wallace should insist upon it in justice to himself and to the gallant men who so valiantly fought of the Third Division as to hold an enemy so greatly outnumbering us at bay for almost an entire day.

If General Lee knew the *facts* in the premises it would not redound to General Early's military valor, genius or judgment so far as his conduct of this battle is concerned, any way. He ought to have driven us from the field at once, and would with his usual dash. Had he done so, he might capture Washington and may now if other troops haven't been sent from the Army of the Potomac, but I'm sure they have. The enemy is estimated at 20,000 strong. At any rate it is many times our size as I could see it from a hilltop where I was during a part of the battle. We are falling back over the pike to the Relay House.

General Early says in his "Memoirs" in regard to this fight: "McCausland, crossing the river with his brigade, dismounted his men and advanced rapidly against the enemy's left flank, which he threw into confusion, but he was then gradually forced back. McCausland's movement, which was brilliantly executed, solved the problem for me, and orders were sent to Breckenridge to move up rapidly with Gordon's Division to McCausland's assistance, and, striking the enemy's left, drive him from the position commanding the crossings in Ramseur's front, so that the latter might cross. The Division crossed under the personal superintendence of General Breckenridge, and, while Ramseur skirmished with the enemy in front,"—which didn't deceive us at all—"the attack was made by Gordon in gallant style, and with the aid of several pieces of King's artillery, which had been crossed over, and Nelson's artillery from the opposite side, he threw the enemy into great confusion and forced him from his position, Ramseur immediately crossed on the railroad bridge and pursued the enemy's flying forces; and Rhodes crossed on the left and joined in the pursuit. Between six hundred and seven hundred unwounded prisoners fell into their hands, and the enemy's loss in killed and wounded was very heavy. Our loss in killed and wounded was about seven hundred. The action closed about sunset."

According to General Grant's "Memoirs," Early's command at this time consisted of four divisions or twenty brigades, composed of the very sinew or hardened veterans made so from the constant fighting of sixty-five depleted regiments of infantry, three brigades of cavalry and three battalions of artillery since the commencement of the war. It must be taken into consideration, too, that the corps, divisions and brigades of the Confederate army were just as big again when its army was reorganized in 1863, as ours. The foregoing does not include the brigades of infantry composing Breckenridge's division as its composition is unknown to me, but all of which confronted us on some part of the field together with the other foregoing mentioned organizations. At one time we were fighting in our two fronts to our left center, facing southerly and westerly, forty-five infantry regiments and more, McCausland's brigade of dismounted cavalry, and several pieces if not all of Nelson's and King's artillery either on one side of the river or the other; fourteen of which infantry regiments were with Ramseur on our west front across the river and thirty-one with Gordon in our south front near the Thomas house on the east side of the river behind which a line of McCausland's dismounted cavalry was formed by Gordon, after it was defeated in its first assault.

Although General Early admits that it took until about sunset to fairly dispose of us, it being then mid-summer when the days are about the longest of the year, what he says as a whole, in some respects is misleading. He did not at once rout us as soon as Gordon's assault commenced at about 3 o'clock p. m. as even with the help of McCausland's brigade and Nelson's and King's artillery he was repulsed, when he says himself he asked twice that another brigade be sent him from the west side of the river and even then after getting it he was held in check some time when, General Rhodes having forced a crossing on our right at or near the Baltimore pike, and having to weaken our line at the railroad bridge to reinforce our line in front of Gordon, we were so weak that a retreat was ordered, being fast surrounded, but we didn't give up until told to. The Ninth Regiment of New York Heavy Artillery, one Hundred and Sixth, One Hundred and Tenth, One Hundred and Twenty-sixth and One Hundred and Fifty-first Regiments of New York Infantry, and the Fourteenth New Jersey not being fortunate as was the Tenth Vermont in finding natural breastworks in their front at first, their casualties were larger than in the other regiments or at least than in the Tenth Vermont. General Tyler's command lost one officer and fourteen enlisted men killed, four officers and seventy-nine enlisted men wounded, seven officers and one hundred and sixteen enlisted men were captured or missing, making a total of two hundred and twenty-one casualties all told in that command. Early levied a contribution of $200,000 on Frederick, burnt Governor Bradford's suburban residence, Postmaster-General Blair's home at Silver Springs, in the suburbs of Washington, D. C., and later Chambersburg and Williamsport, as well as other small places which did not pay tribute in money.

General Gordon, when speaking of this fight to a survivor on the Union side afterwards, stated that it was one of the hardest fights he saw during the war and he was in many, many of them. A division of his command and

McCausland's brigade confronted six or more regiments of the Third Division, including the Tenth Vermont, and still the enemy here had to be reinforced. Let us hope that Time, our kindliest and truest friend in all things but One, will yet place the brilliant little Battle of the Monocacy in history before the world as it belongs.

General Grant in his "Personal Memoirs" makes this interesting reference to Monocacy: "The force under General Wallace was small in numbers to move against Early. The situation in Washington was precarious. Wallace moved with commendable promptitude and met the enemy at Monocacy. He could hardly have expected to gain a victory, but hoped to cripple and delay the enemy until Washington could be put in a state of preparation to meet Early. With Rickett's Division at Monocacy on time, Wallace succeeded in stopping Early for the day on which the battle took place.

"The next morning Early started on his march to the capital of the Nation, arriving before it on the 11th. Learning of the gravity of the situation, I ordered Meade to send the other two Divisions of the Sixth Corps to Washington for the relief of the city. The latter reached there the very day that Early arrived before it. The Nineteenth Corps, under General Emory, arrived in Washington from Fort Monroe about the same time.

"Early made his reconnoissance with the view of attacking the city on the 12th, but the next morning he found intrenchments fully manned. He commenced to retreat, with the Sixth Corps following. There is no telling how much this result was contributed to by General Lew Wallace's leading at Monocacy what might well have been considered almost a forlorn hope. If Early had been but one day sooner, he might have entered the capital before the arrival of the forces I had sent there.

"Whether the delay caused by the battle amounted to a day or not, General Wallace contributed on this occasion a greater benefit to the cause than often falls to the lot of a commander of an equal force to render by means of a victory."

One would get the impression from the foregoing, that the whole of Rickett's Division was engaged at Monocacy. It was not. Two and a half regiments or more, I was credibly informed at the time and have been since, was in a train of cars eight miles to the rear as before stated. The reason for this, it was said, was because the engineer refused to go with the train any nearer the front; but, if so, why not have marched, or better still, have compelled the engineer at the point of a bayonet and loaded gun to have taken the train to the front? Surely the commanding officer of that force could not have been a model soldier or man of force, and much less an ardent, devoted patriot, in this instance.

According to Dr. E. M. Haynes' History of the Tenth Vermont, the Union loss in killed, wounded and missing in this fight was 1,294, of which 1,072 were of Rickett's Third Division of the Sixth Corps. There were eleven officers and five hundred and forty-nine enlisted men taken prisoners, thirty-five officers and five hundred and seventy-five enlisted men wounded and ten officers and one hundred and thirteen enlisted men killed. Early mentions the killed and wounded of his command in his official report as "about" seven hundred, which was about the same as ours, showing when the strength of the two commands is taken into consideration, about three to one, how desperately our force contested every inch of ground at Monocacy in this fight. The Third Division lost fully one-fourth or more of its men engaged. General Ricketts, one of the best fighting generals in the army and much beloved by his men, commanded the Third Division, Sixth Corps and was second in command to General Wallace of all the forces there.

The Battle of the Monocacy for obvious reasons, was one of the most stubbornly contested fights and the most important in its result of any I was in during the war. It is remarkable when it is taken into consideration that the Union force of about 5,850 men—of whom about 2,500 had never fired a gun in real battle—and seven pieces of artillery, with no trains or reserve ammunition of any kind, not even a newspaper reporter, so suddenly by reason of Early's invasion had everything come about, could fight from 8 o'clock a. m. to 5 o'clock p. m., a force of from 15,000 to 20,000 of Lee's veterans, and about forty pieces of field artillery with plenty of ammunition, under such a dashing, strategic commander as General Early. But through the grace of God, it is thought he was over-cautious in this fight; he had lost his accustomed dash. It will ever be a disputed point, however, exactly how many men Early had, as twenty-five years after the battle General Lomax who was in it under Early, informed me that many of Early's organizations had been so reduced from constant fighting in the summer's campaign, that even regiments with but few men left were commanded by non-commissioned officers who made no morning reports and that the exact strength of Early's force was unknown. Lomax placed it under 13,000 all told, but I think it was more.

Great credit is due General Wallace for his excellent judgment in his selection of a battlefield, as but for that to have fought against such odds, whatever it was, would have been folly outside the strong fortifications of Washington; but Baltimore had to be protected, too, which necessitated the Battle of the Monocacy. Wallace should have been commended in orders and thanked by Congress for his splendid judgment and pluck to confront such an overwhelming force as well as for the indirect benefits which resulted from his having had the intrepidity to undertake, from a purely military viewpoint, as Grant says "almost a forlorn hope"; but instead of this he was ignominiously treated by General Halleck because Wallace's command had not accomplished an impossibility, it is presumed, by defeating Early. It should be vigorously resented in history by every honest, fairminded man who is an advocate of fair play, and especially by the surviving members of that intrepid little army, discredited by General Halleck by his treatment of Wallace, the stubbornness of which army, according to General Gordon's official report of the fight, caused the waters of the Monocacy to run red with the mingled blood of the blue and the gray on that memorable day when it fought not only to save the National Capital, but to prevent the disastrous moral and other effects its loss would have produced, and the comfort it would have given to northern copperheads, allies of the Confederacy, and especially to the enemy wherever found. If Washington had fallen into the hands of the enemy, even though only temporarily, at this time, it would of course have been sacked and its public buildings destroyed; Grant's plan of campaign, even if it hadn't put an end to his military career, might have been changed, the Confederacy might possibly have been recognized by foreign powers—for it is no small matter for an enemy to occupy a belligerent's capital—and the war might have been somewhat prolonged, if nothing more.

The ovation given that part of Rickett's Division of the famous historic fighting Sixth Corps, which bore the brunt of the Monocacy infantry fighting, as it marched up Pennsylvania Avenue a few days later, and especially the bullet, shell, weather-beaten and battle-torn flags of the Tenth Vermont, as they appeared along the line of march, is a proud and pleasant memory never to be forgotten. It was the event of the day, no other regiment within hearing, receiving such a continuous and noisy reception. It will go with the men of that most excellent regiment throughout eternity; it was a proud day. The regiment had been one of the most valiant of some nine or more in the Monocacy fight to save the capital; it was known in Washington and it was pleasant to feel the city understood and appreciated it. It has never been thought, though, by the survivors of the command who fought in the Monocacy battle that the general public did appreciate, or has since appreciated it, as a defeat is generally looked upon as a disaster and with discredit; but indirectly in this case it was a great victory, one of the most important of the war for obvious reasons aside from having saved the National Capital, as without the delay of a day or more, caused by this fight. Early certainly would have found no veteran troops to defend the city, for even as it was some of them had to double quick through the city—a fact not before given in history it is believed—into line of battle just north of it at Fort Stevens from the transports which had brought them from in front of Petersburg to fight Early whose appearance before the city they were just in season to confront with hardly a moment to spare. Says Hon. L. E. Chittenden, Registrar of the Treasury in his "Recollections of President Lincoln and his

Administration": "The importance of a battle is determined by its ultimate consequences rather than its immediate results. If that fought on the Monocacy did delay General Early so as to save the capital from his assault and probable capture, it was one of the decisive battles of the world." Thus we have the matter summed up here in barely two sentences for it did delay Early just enough to save the capital.

This was forty years ago this 9th day of July, 1904, when many of the survivors, including myself, have been celebrating the anniversary of the Monocacy fight at Frederick, Md., and on the battlefield; and even now old department clerks who largely formed the Home Guard in 1864, and were in the trenches in front of Washington when Early approached the city, mention with wonder the apparent indifference and yet alertness with which the veteran Sixth Corps skirmish line double quicked from in front of the works to meet and repulse Early's advance. They did it in a matter of fact way, it seemed to the clerks, as though going to the drill ground in time of peace for manoeuvres. Those were days though, when we fought with clenched teeth, and learned to smother our emotions. We had no time to growl over rations, as in the Spanish-American War, in more recent times, and did not murmur if at times we got but a hard tack a day and nothing else and most of the men not even that, as at Mine Run, and many other places. We were in the field to preserve the Union and to eliminate the National parasite of human slavery, and constant fighting had taught every man who from conscientious motives could always be found when well, on the fighting line and nowhere else, exactly what to do under most circumstances; and hence, they were generally cool having thoroughly learned the science of war.

SUNDAY, July 10, 1864.

Oh! I'm so tired and used up I can hardly write; have been marching all day on the pike, and my feet are badly blistered, besides being so lame, sore and stiff from my wound I can hardly move without groaning and crying out with pain after being still a little while. We arrived at Ellicott's Mills, Md., about 4 o'clock p. m. where we remained about two hours and took the cars for the Relay House. The Sixty-seventh Pennsylvania is with us. The balance of the division is yet at the mills. Stragglers still continue to pour in. Our regiment was never before in such disorder, i. e. so many stragglers. The tension was so great though, having held the enemy all day with such an attenuated line, that when it did collapse, being nearly surrounded, it was every man for himself in order to keep from being captured. The stragglers report the enemy's cavalry close after them all along the retreat in order to pick up prisoners. We arrived at the Relay House at sundown with only about ninety men. But the regiment fought valiantly yesterday up to the last moment when we were obliged to fall back in disorder or be made prisoners of war, and anybody could have played checkers on my coat-tail, I know, if they could have kept up, for Libby Prison had terrors for me, and I have always looked upon it as being a disgrace to be taken prisoner by the enemy; but in this I am wrong—*still* it would hurt my pride to be captured. We found no troops but a regiment of hundred days' men here, and they were greatly frightened. We are camped a short distance in rear of the hotel on a side hill in the woods.

Monday, July 11, 1864.

We shall probably remain here several days and rest; am stiff and do not feel like moving on account of my bruise which is all black and sore and my hip is stiff. It's reported the enemy is close by Baltimore. The greatest excitement prevails accordingly, among citizens, and for fear communication will be cut with Washington. We can hear everything except reliable news. I've arrived at that stage where nothing excites me, I've been through so much in the last seventy days.

Tuesday, July 12, 1864.

Still the Tenth and Sixty-seventh regiments are allowed to remain undisturbed by the enemy while it is having things pretty much its own way in the vicinity of Baltimore and Washington. It's reported this evening Gilmore's rebel cavalry have burned the Gunpowder Bridge, destroyed a railroad train, robbed the passengers, etc. The greatest consternation prevails throughout the country, as the enemy is reported to be only three miles from the National Capital. We wait anxiously for the next news.

Wednesday, July 13, 1864.

Good! I have been looking for it! The First and Second Divisions of the Sixth Corps arrived in Washington last night just in season by double quicking through the city from the boats to drive the enemy from the fortifications; can hear heavy guns in that direction this morning; don't know what the difficulty is but if the rest of our Corps is there the Johnnies will never take the capital, and we are all right. Hurrah! I am on picket to-day at Mr. Donaldson's, a wealthy Union man who has a lovely home and family. This is an aristocratic neighborhood, and people embarrass me with their courteous attentions. I would much rather be left to myself, for I'm tired and haven't anything with me but the clothes worn through so many battles, besmeared, ragged, riddled with bullets and torn by exploding shells; so I am not dressed to appear at table with conventional people; but still they insist upon it, and what plagues me more make a lion of me. Oh dear! I'd rather make an assault on such a place as the "Bloody Angle" at Spottsylvania! The young ladies are awfully pretty, so nice and attentive, too, that I feel overwhelmed. I'm not sensible enough, though, not to wish myself somewhere else, for I'm dirty and unpresentable. It's truly a sunny spot in a soldier's life, though, to run across such families occasionally when presentable. General Tyler has come in to-night; all's quiet.

THURSDAY, July 14, 1864.

Major Dillingham, with a detachment of the Eighty-seventh Pennsylvania, went through on the train tonight to Washington to open the railroad. There is no truth in the report that the road was torn up. We took the cars at the Relay House at 11 o'clock a. m. and arrived in Washington at 3 o'clock p. m. The excitement has mostly subsided in the city. The rest of our Corps is reported at Poolesville, Md. We stay in Washington to-night.

FRIDAY, July 15, 1864.

Remained in camp until 8 o'clock a. m. and then marched up Pennsylvania Avenue by the Treasury, White House and War Department, amidst a continuous ovation for fully three miles. Great respect was shown our Division, as it was known that it was its stubborn fighting at Monocacy that had saved Washington, and the sidewalks, windows, balconies, housetops, etc., were thronged with enthusiastic people. The business-like appearance of our regiment, its proud bearing, fine cadence and marching, its weather-beaten, tattered old battle flags all in strings from shot and shell, as well as the men's clothes, its splendid band, together with the evergreen sprig proudly worn by some of us, which always gains us recognition, captured the crowd, and the heartiness of our deserved ovation over all other regiments in line was very noticeable. It was a proud day for the plucky Tenth Vermont, never to be forgotten—even prouder than when showered with flowers on our return home at Burlington a year later—for we were the feature of the parade—real live heroic Green Mountain Boys, as true and valiant as was ever Ethan Allen. We had a right to be proud, for hadn't we proved to the world many times what Meade said to us at Spottsylvania and Sedgwick at the Wilderness, when some wag said to Meade at Spottsylvania when in rear of our regiment, as the lines were being hastily formed for assault on the enemy a stone's throw away, that he was in a dangerous place, and he replied, "I'm safe enough behind a Vermont regiment, anywhere?" We marched via Georgetown and Tennallytown to within a few miles of Offutt's crossroads and bivouacked. It is rumored that we are to join our corps at Poolesville. Probably we shall have to chase the enemy down the Shenandoah Valley again. As the Sixth Corps is the best marching, fighting and most reliable one in the army, I reckon Grant and Meade knew what they were about when they concluded to send it after Early. Now, if they will only send us Sheridan, we will lick the whole rebel army if they will set it on to us in detail, and finish up the war.

SATURDAY, July 16, 1864.

Arrived at the crossroads about dark and camped for the night. Lieut. Merritt Barber and I went on a scout for some supper, but couldn't find much, as the rebels have taken everything in the country. The men are very tired; arrived at the Potomac about dark and waded the river two miles below Edward's Ferry at Young's Island; are in camp for the night on the Leesburg pike just on the south side of Goose Creek. The rest of the Sixth Corps is at Leesburg.

Sunday, July 17, 1864.

Oh, such a horrid night's rest! Being near the mountains it was cold with a heavy dew, and I had nothing but a rubber poncho for cover, and am not feeling very well in consequence of being so chilled after marching all day in the hot sun. We marched at 7 o'clock and arrived at Leesburg at 8 o'clock a. m., where we rested an hour. We found Col. Stephen Thomas here with the Eighth Vermont Infantry, now of the Nineteenth Corps. The balance of our Corps was about two miles ahead, and we overtook it at 6 o'clock p. m. and are camped in a shady grove for the night. General H. G. Wright of our Corps is in command of this army now, which numbers about 25,000 men. It is composed of the Sixth Corps, two Divisions of the Nineteenth Corps under General Emery, and General George Crook's Eighth Corps of about 7,000 men, which has operated largely in West Virginia and the Shenandoah Valley.

Monday, July 18, 1864.

Marched at 4 o'clock a. m., passed through Snickersville on a narrow stony road, and arrived at Snicker's Gap about noon. We went through the gap, but on arriving at the Shenandoah river at Island Ford about 6 o'clock p. m. found that some of Crook's force had crossed and was skirmishing; did not fight very well; fell back to the river in a stampede, plunged in and some were drowned; probably green troops. Mosby's guerillas have been in our rear all day and robbed some of our stragglers. The artillery shelling this evening made us feel uncomfortable, as the shells landed right among us.

Tuesday, July 19, 1864.

The enemy did not press us further than the river last night, nor have they made an advance to-day, yet they remain in our front. They are busy caring for their wounded. Both sides are within shelling distance; have remained in our works all day which we built last night.

Wednesday, July 20, 1864.

We shelled the enemy about 3 o'clock a. m. It left our front during the night. We crossed the river about noon to-day, marched about four miles and halted in a hard thunder shower. We fell in soon and the Sixth and Nineteenth Corps started on our back track, supposedly for Petersburg via Washington. General

Crook's Corps followed Early on up the Shenandoah Valley.

THURSDAY, July 21, 1864.

Marched hard all night and daylight found us nearly through the gap; have marched hard—fairly raced—all day; brought up on the east side of Goose Creek again, where we are in camp for the night tired and worn out. We marched through Leesburg with stars and stripes waving and bands playing national airs, something unusual for us to do without it's a large place. Rumor says that our rear guard burned the place, but I don't believe it, although it has the reputation of being strongly rebel—a regular hotbed.

FRIDAY, July 22, 1864.

The Tenth Vermont has been train guard to-day; marched reasonably; are in camp east of Difficult Creek for the night. Yesterday a boy soldier was shot down in cold blood by a guerilla within sight of the ambulance corps; only heard of it to-day.

SATURDAY, July 23, 1864.

I was awakened at 4 o'clock and told the Corps would march at 4.30 o'clock p. m., but it didn't till much later. We are train guard again to-day; crossed the Chain Bridge at 3 o'clock p. m. and camped just below Tennallytown on the Georgetown pike. Major Harper is paying off some of the troops. Probably we shall be paid before we go to Petersburg, but rumors are such we may not go. Early has driven Crook back to Martinsburg with loss.

SUNDAY, July 24, 1864.

Have been in camp resting all day. Adjutant Lyman is fixing up the pay rolls. I can't find my valise; guess it's lost. We had inspection at 10 a. m.; cloudy; looks like rain.

MONDAY, July 25, 1864.

Got supper in town last night. It began to rain about 10 o'clock p. m. and continued to hard all night. I stayed at the National Hotel; went to camp early this morning; regiment paid last night; went to town again and bought clothes; went to the Canterbury Theatre in the evening; stayed at the National Hotel again. There's no sign of a move to-night.

TUESDAY, July 26, 1864.

I was aroused early this morning by Major Dillingham, who said the army had moved at daylight. I engaged a hack and went up to camp, but found everything as we left it. We marched at 9 o'clock a. m. for Rockville; passed through the town just before dark and camped for the night about two miles out on the Rockville road. I have called on the Henning, Higgins and Dr. Stonestreet families; enjoyed the visits greatly. These families were very kind to me in the winter of 1862-63 when ill with typhoid fever; splendid people. General Crook's back on the Maryland side of the Potomac again and Early's forces are raiding the country again, too.

Wednesday, July 27, 1864.

Marched about 5 o'clock a. m.; took a crossroad and went to the Rockville and Alexandria pike; hard march; camped at Hyattstown; are headed for Frederick Junction on the Monocacy River, where we had our fight July 9, 1864.

Thursday, July 28, 1864.

Very dry; no prospect of rain; wish we might have some; marched at 6 o'clock a. m. for Frederick Junction; band played as we passed through Urbana; arrived at the Junction at 1 o'clock p. m.; remained about two hours and marched for Jefferson City; arrived there at 11 o'clock p. m. and camped.

Friday, July 29, 1864.

Marched at 7 o'clock a. m. for Harper's Ferry; passed through the town about noon and camped on the Winchester pike about two miles to the south; warm and sultry; am not well to-night; hope to get a day's rest here; all's quiet, except rumors of Early's raiders.

Saturday, July 30, 1864.

Oh, it's been *so* warm! I do wish we could have some rain, it would be so refreshing! We remained in camp until 3 o'clock p. m., when it was reported the enemy was passing through South Mountain, and of course we had to "get." Our brigade is train guard; got a large mail to-night. My commission came as First Lieutenant of Company E, Tenth Vermont, but I cannot get mustered, as Captain Smith, our mustering officer, is in Washington.

Sunday, July 31, 1864.

Remained on Bolivar Heights last night; regiment went on picket about 10 o'clock p. m.; train mostly crossed the river last night, but did not all move till near noon to-day; heat intense, but haven't marched hard. The train, as anticipated, did not go further than Sandy Hook, as the mules were completely fagged out, so our brigade was ordered to join the Corps which is at Frederick; camped at Jefferson City. We were startled yesterday afternoon when half-way up the mountain, by the explosion of a magazine filled with ammunition. The report was alarming and was followed by a shower of stones, gravel, sticks, pieces of shell and dirt which was very demoralizing, besides, we didn't know what to make of it at first. It gave us quite a scare; suspected a mine at first.

Many men have had sunstrokes and died to-day.

MONDAY, Aug. 1, 1864.

Marched for Frederick at 5 o'clock a. m.; dusty and hot; arrived at 9 o'clock a. m.; camped in a shady grove; Chambersburg reported burnt by the enemy because it couldn't or wouldn't meet a levy by McCausland of $500,000 in currency; also that Grant has blown up a sixteen-gun battery and taken one complete line of works; have been mustered today; took command of Company E as First Lieutenant of that Company.

TUESDAY, Aug. 2, 1864.

Have remained in camp; rest much appreciated; have written Dr. Almon Clark. It's reported to-night that Grant fell back again to-day to his old position; also reported that forty families here in Frederick who sympathize with the rebels are to leave for the South in the morning; don't believe it; can hear all sorts of improbable things when so much excitement prevails.

WEDNESDAY, Aug. 3, 1864.

Received orders to march at 5 o'clock a. m., but as we were train guard we did not move till 7 o'clock a. m.; camped at 1 o'clock p. m. near Buckeystown at Monocacy Mill on the Monocacy river; bathed in the river; all's quiet to-night.

THURSDAY, Aug 4, 1864.

Remained in camp all day; services were held today over the remains of the First Division Inspector; various rumors about moving.

FRIDAY, Aug. 5, 1864.

Received marching orders at 4 o'clock a. m. to be ready to move at 5 o'clock, and thus it has been all day, but night finds us still in the same camp. It's rumored our pickets were driven in last night at Harper's Ferry. I have pitched my tent and made arrangements to stay all night, which is the only indication of a move; generally move when I do this.

SATURDAY, Aug. 6, 1864.

As I expected, I hadn't more than nicely gotten asleep when the bugle sounded the assembly, and in less than thirty minutes we were on the march for Frederick Junction; arrived there about midnight; got orders to make ourselves comfortable for two hours, and then take the cars for Harper's Ferry, but did not start until about noon; saw Grant at the Junction; looks like fighting ahead; is probably arranging the campaign in his car with others.

SUNDAY, Aug. 7, 1864.

This morning found us in line about two miles outside of Harper's Ferry, but no signs of an enemy in our immediate front; has been quite warm all day; have written Pert and Will Clark; most of the regiments have had dress parade, but Colonel Henry can't see it quite yet that way. It is rumored that General Sheridan is to command this army—good!

MONDAY, Aug. 8, 1864.

All quiet in camp to-day. Lieut. D. G. Hill and Sergt. J. M. Read's commissions came this afternoon. Lieut. Hill has been mustered; haven't done much but read Harper's Weekly and visit; baggage came up this evening; warm and sultry; rumors of a move to-night; men have been enjoying themselves to-day.

TUESDAY, Aug. 9, 1864.

Am making out muster and pay rolls; got a letter from J. R. Seaver and another from Aunt Nancy Merrill of Chelsea, Vt. Lieut. J. M. Read reported to his Company for duty this afternoon. Captain L. D. Thompson and Lieut. G. E. Davis have gone on picket this evening; good news from Sherman and the Gulf Department to-night; rumors of a move this evening.

WEDNESDAY, Aug. 10, 1864.

Marched this morning at 5 o'clock about fifteen miles to Charlestown, West Virginia, and camped about three miles from Berryville at Clifton; very warm; many fell out from sunstroke and heat; rained this evening; no signs of the enemy.

THURSDAY, Aug. 11, 1864.

Marched at 6 o'clock a. m. Our regiment has been train guard; cavalry has had warm work in the locality of Winchester, Va., as considerable cannonading has been heard in that vicinity. We are camped on the same ground the rebs were on last night; should judge we were making for Manassas Gap by the course we are taking; made an easy march to-day.

FRIDAY, Aug. 12, 1864.

Another day still finds us marching in dust and under a scorching sun. The heat has indeed been intense. Many a poor soldier has fallen out on the way from exhaustion and sunstroke. We have passed through Newtown and Middletown, both of which were nearly deserted, and those left are bitter secessionists. We have been chasing the enemy, which accounts for our marching so hard; its rear guard left Newtown as we entered it. We camped for dinner here and to wait for stragglers to catch up.

An amusing thing occurred here. Three young officers, Lieutenants D. G. Hill,

G. P. Welch and myself, went to the only hotel to get dinner, but found the front door locked and the blinds all drawn. The back yard and garden containing vegetables, fruit trees, flowers, etc., in luxuriance, was inclosed by a high brick wall about eight feet high with an entrance on a side street. A matronly-looking attendant unlocked the door at our request, and admitted us to the garden and back door of the hotel, which stood open to the kitchen, which we entered, the attendant remaining within hearing. Here we found the landlady, who declared in an assumed, distressed manner that she had nothing in the house to eat, the enemy having taken everything she had, at the same time relating a tale of woe which I presumed might be partially true, if not wholly so. Soon, however, after parleying, she produced a plate of fine hot tea biscuit, nervously forcing them into our very faces, saying, "Have biscuit! have biscuit!" which, rest assured, we did.

After this I started to leave. The colored woman who had admitted us, having heard all that was said, hid by the corner of the house en route to the garden entrance, and when I passed shyly told me that a table in the parlor where the curtains were down, was loaded down with a steaming hot dinner with the best the house afforded, prepared for a party of rebel officers who had fled about when it was ready because of the approach of our army. I returned to the kitchen bound to have that dinner just because it had been prepared for rebel officers and told the landlady what I had discovered, and that we *must* have that dinner, but were willing to pay her for it. Seeing she was outmanoeuvered and that her duplicity was discovered, she looked scared and laughing nervously led the way to the parlor, where we found the table actually groaning with steaming viands as though prepared for and awaiting us. She graciously bade us be seated, presided at the table with dignity and grace as though nothing had happened, and we met her with equal suavity, laughter and dignity as though she was the greatest lady living, she admitting when through, that she had had a "real good time." We paid for the dinner and parted good friends.

SATURDAY, Aug. 13, 1864.

Well, were it natural for me to be despondent, I should say that things looked rather gloomy for our cause. I do not doubt but what General Grant is doing all in his power to prosecute the war. Apparently, however, there is little doubt but what there are those under him who fail to perform their whole duty. If there were only more fighting generals and fewer get-along-easy fellows, what a splendid thing it would be for the country. But Grant will weed 'em out in time —see if he don't! We arrived at Cedar Creek and went about a mile when we again found Early in our front; have remained here all day.

SUNDAY, Aug 14, 1864.

Have remained idle all day; enemy occupy the other side of Strasburg. Our pickets are just this side of town; very warm and sultry; are in the shade. Captain Merritt Barber and Lieut. J. M. Read have gone on picket; no skirmishing to-day; rations and mail expected to-night.

MONDAY, Aug. 15, 1864.

Have remained quietly in camp to-day; skirmishing and artillery firing along the line this afternoon; warm, but cooler than yesterday; army moved back across Cedar Creek about 9 o'clock a. m. to our old position; wagons have come, but have got to make three days' rations last four, as Mosby captured some of our train; all's quiet to-night.

TUESDAY, Aug. 16, 1864.

Such trifling! I'm tired of it! Must be we are waiting for something—aren't ready. I am glad to lay quiet, but such suspense keeps us from resting. We can't depend on quiet. It's rumored we are to fall back this evening. Quite a game of chess seems to be going on between the armies. It has been very dull since we left Harper's Ferry. We have done nothing but march without mail and time drags; are nearly out of rations.

WEDNESDAY, Aug. 17, 1864.

We were ordered to commence our retrograde movement at 8.30 o'clock, but didn't till about 10 o'clock a. m. As usual our division goes as train guard. We passed through Middletown about midnight; didn't stop to do much foraging; arrived at Newtown about 2 o'clock a. m., and passing through, the men nearly stripping the place of everything; got breakfast at Winchester and stopped near Clifton farm. Foraging is allowed, owing to the levies made for money on places by the enemy, which if not paid have been burnt, in Maryland and Pennsylvania, such as Williamsport, Chambersburg, etc. It is desired, too, to strip the Shenandoah Valley of all supplies in order to keep the enemy out of it.

THURSDAY, Aug. 18, 1864.

The enemy followed us and overtook our rear guard at Winchester where Generals Torbert and Wilson and the New Jersey brigade of the Sixth Corps had a sharp little fight last night losing it's said, one hundred and eighty in killed, wounded and prisoners. We were aroused to form line of battle this morning at 4 o'clock. We got breakfast and marched about 6 o'clock a. m. It rained constantly all forenoon and was lowering this afternoon; dined at Clifton farm; marched to Charlestown and bivouacked at 9 o'clock p. m. We have got to make three days' rations last five.

FRIDAY, Aug. 19, 1864.

Arose at a late hour this morning, but not in the best of spirits; have been in camp all day; haven't made preparations to stay long; don't now-a-days; can't tell what we are to do; rained early, but broke away by noon; have been quite indisposed since 3 o'clock p. m.; fear I'm going to be ill; got a letter from Pert this evening; first mail received in a week; all's quiet on the line to-night.

SATURDAY, Aug. 20, 1864.

Arose early this morning and am feeling better; over-tired yesterday from hard marching and fatigue, I reckon, was all; took an early breakfast and soon learned my baggage was close at hand; put up my tent and got ready for work to-morrow provided we stay here; put in a requisition for clothing. Lieut. C. H. Reynolds, R. Q. M. has come from City Point; have written to Dr. J. H. Jones this evening; all's quiet.

SUNDAY, Aug. 21, 1864.

Well, a soldier's life is a strange one to lead! I got up about 8 o'clock a. m. received an order for inspection at 9 o'clock a. m. got nearly ready when it commenced raining and inspection was delayed. Then before we had inspection about 10 o'clock a. m. a lively fusilade commenced on the pike in our front with the skirmishers; looks to me like a surprise; everybody acts so, too; have been hustling all day to throw up rifle pits and to-night finds us in line behind a formidable breastwork; skirmishing still continues briskly. The Vermont brigade reestablished the skirmish line. Our brigade has lost two men killed and eleven wounded.

MONDAY, Aug. 22, 1864.

Am not feeling well; marched nearly all night; arrived at Halltown heights at daylight; went into our old position; am now on picket on the right of our line; enemy followed us up and skirmished with our rear guard "right smart" all day. About 11 o'clock a. m. the First Division was sent out on the pike; rumored it's driven the enemy back; hard thunderstorm from 3 o'clock to 4 o'clock p. m.; quite cool this evening.

TUESDAY, Aug. 23, 1864.

It was chilly and foggy this morning, but it cleared about 9 o'clock a. m. Skirmishing still continues on the pike and on the left of the line. It's rumored the Nineteenth Corps charged the enemy this morning driving it back in confusion. The Tenth Vermont moved to the right this forenoon giving room for a battery on our left. Our forces have thrown up breastworks, but I don't anticipate any attack.

WEDNESDAY, Aug. 24, 1864.

This is my twenty-second birthday; enemy still in front; skirmishing still on the left; don't think it amounts to much; heavy cannonading in front of the Nineteenth Corps from 2 o'clock to 3 o'clock p. m. Dr. Almon Clark and Lieutenant E. P. Farr returned to the regiment to-day. I have been busy on clothing rolls and Company books and wrote to James Burnham this evening; not feeling well to-day; very warm; all's quiet.

THURSDAY, Aug. 25, 1864.

Well, another birthday has passed and with it another year has gone, and one of great military experience, and I trust it has been profitably spent; very warm till about 3 o'clock p. m. when it showered; had monthly inspection at 4 o'clock p. m. General Wilson's division of cavalry started this morning on a reconnoissance towards Martinsburg; heard heavy cannonading about 3 o'clock p. m.; can't learn any particulars.

FRIDAY, Aug. 26, 1864.

As usual we were ordered to be under arms at 4 o'clock a. m. but the enemy has not yet appeared on our right, nor do I think they will; have had charge of a fatigue party nearly all day policing in front of the rifle pits. Captain L. T. Hunt of Company H returned to the regiment this afternoon looking well; has been absent wounded. Captains C. D. Bogue and A. W. Chilton's commissions came by to-day's mail; no skirmishing all day.

SATURDAY, Aug. 27, 1864.

Were under arms again early this morning. Colonel Foster visited the Tenth this forenoon; is truly a fine-looking man. I have been very busy making out final statements. The heavy musketry heard yesterday on our left about 3 o'clock p. m. was occasioned by the enemy's making a charge on the Nineteenth Corps. The Johnnies were repulsed with considerable loss. Rumor says we captured one entire regiment and two stand of colors, etc. It's child's play, though, compared to the fighting from the Rapidan to the James. I don't believe there will be any more such fighting; it's more than human beings can stand without one side or the other collapsing. As I look back upon it, I marvel.

SUNDAY, Aug. 28, 1864.

Received marching orders for to-morrow morning at 10 o'clock last evening. We were up at 3 o'clock a. m. and ready to march at daylight, but did not until near 8 o'clock. The Nineteenth Corps marched on our left in three different columns and the Sixth Corps moved on the right in the same order. We took dinner about two miles from Charlestown, and marched again about 1 o'clock p. m.; went through Charlestown about 3 o'clock p. m., with the bands playing

"Old John Brown" to the accompanying chorus of the entire column. It was grand! We camped on our old ground just outside the city; no signs of any enemy yet.

Monday, Aug. 29, 1864.

A cool comfortable day; laid out Company streets this forenoon and everything looks as though we were to remain in camp several days. Torbet's cavalry has been engaged all day, but was driven back about 4 o'clock when our Division was sent out to support it. The enemy fell back as soon as they discovered our infantry. We followed the rebs about five miles, returned about half way to camp, and bivouacked. There's good news from Grant's army to-night. We await anxiously for the returns from the Chicago convention.

Tuesday, Aug. 30, 1864.

We were under arms at 3 o'clock a. m., but no signs of an enemy. It's a beautiful cool morning. Some think Early has gone to reinforce Lee; guess not; at any rate, an enemy is in front. The Third Division hasn't moved back to its original position as anticipated last night. Time hangs heavily and were it not for the bands I should be almost homesick; got a mail but no news from home.

Wednesday, Aug. 31, 1864.

Pleasant and warm; got our muster and pay rolls this morning; completed two; not much skirmishing to-day; paper states that probably General McClellan will be the Democratic nominee for president; got a mail but no letter for me.

Thursday, Sept. 1, 1864.

This is the anniversary of our muster into the U. S. service at Brattleboro, Vt., 1862. Thus far, as a regiment, we have been prospered. God grant that we may continue to be, and that as many as is consistent with His will, may be allowed to pass one more year if necessary in the service, and then be returned home happy, feeling that we have endeavored to do our duty as soldiers faithfully to our country and our God; have completed two more rolls; shall try and finish the other in the morning; all's quiet in front.

Friday, Sept. 2, 1864.

Cloudy and cool; think it will rain in a day or so; have completed my roll. Lieutenant George P. Welch returned from Vermont this afternoon; has been absent sick since we left City Point. We moved back to our old camp at 5 o'clock p. m.; arrived about dark; shall probably stay here several days; are laying out camp.

Saturday, Sept. 3, 1864.

Got an order at 10 o'clock last night to be in readiness to move at 4 o'clock a. m.; didn't start until about 6.30 o'clock a. m.; marched up the valley towards Clifton Farm; did not rest until about three miles of it, and probably shouldn't then had we not run onto the enemy and had a brush; don't know the result; heard to-day Atlanta had fallen. It's glorious news! I was detailed for picket to-night. It looks like rain.

Sunday, Sept. 4, 1864.

Got our line established about 10 o'clock last night; rained hard; got very wet; day has passed quietly; moved our skirmish line about fifty yards to the front this forenoon. The enemy appeared on the left of our division about dark and commenced skirmishing, but all's quiet at 9 o'clock p. m. Dr. Clark has been down to see us this afternoon. He's always welcome. It's cloudy and cool; will probably rain before morning.

Monday, Sept. 5, 1864.

Was aroused this morning at 4 o'clock by the Vermont brigade. It moved round on to our right in the night and built works to protect our right flank; rained hard last night; got very wet; was relieved from picket by the Fourteenth New Jersey; no skirmishing to-day. The enemy has evidently fallen back to Winchester. It's quite cloudy.

Tuesday, Sept. 6, 1864.

O, such a terrible day! Rain, wind, sleet and everything to make it gloomy. The Vermont troops have voted to-day as directed by the Governor. My Company (E) cast seven votes for the Republican candidate. The other men didn't know who the Democratic candidate was and so didn't vote. Nothing has disgusted me so since I left Vermont. I'm sadly disappointed politically, in my Company, but the men are good fighters and I like them. They seem devoted to me. It is disappointing, though, to have to send such a report to Vermont! It's mortifying! But I mustn't let the men know how I feel for it can't be helped now. It makes me feel queer, though, for my Republicanism is as staunch as the granite hill (the Barre granite quarries) on which I was born. I am dazed at the result of the vote in Company E! I guess I'm in the wrong pew politically; very few democrats in Barre.

Wednesday, Sept. 7, 1864.

Was happily surprised to find it pleasant this morning; has turned out the finest day of the fall. Lieutenant H. W. Kingsley came up with the day's rations; ate supper with us. The moonlight, band music and charm of the night has killed the monotony.

Thursday, Sept. 8, 1864.

Such freaky weather; cool and rainy nearly all day. Chaplain Roberts of the Sixth Vermont, has called this afternoon. He's a fine man. I have been reading East Lynne. It's very dull in camp. I've written to Aunt Thompson this evening. The papers state the North is jubilant over our recent victories, and well they may be.

F<small>RIDAY</small>, Sept. 9, 1864.

A fair day. Lieutenant H. W. Kingsley ate supper with us. He brought up three days' rations. Pert writes she is having a fine time in East Boylston, Mass. teaching. She sent me a letter from Cousin Byron Bradley. Cousin Abby Pierce is coming East this fall. I have finished reading East Lynne; it's a fine story.

S<small>ATURDAY</small>, Sept. 10, 1864.

It's a cool day. Company and battalion drill was ordered this afternoon but we didn't drill as the Major is on picket. Lieutenant G. E. Davis came out of the Division hospital this afternoon. He's had a boil. I have made my election returns. It's very pleasant this evening in camp, but dull. I have written Pert.

S<small>UNDAY</small>, Sept. 11, 1864.

A very quiet dull day; am looking for news from the Army of the Potomac; nothing has occurred since we left; those armies watch each other, while we do what little fighting there is done. So much constant chasing of the enemy night and day, frequent brushes, laying on our arms from 3 o'clock till daylight, etc., is very wearing and I shall be glad when Early is licked, as he surely will be for Sheridan fights like a tornado—*he* does things. He's getting a good ready, and we'll be heard from soon. Ta, ta, Early! Run back to Petersburg! The peace party seems to be dissatisfied with McClellan. In my opinion his stock's below par, at the same time if his party nominate a new man it will be the best thing that can happen for us; wonder if most of Company E don't sympathize with the peace party? Hope my men are not fickle politically—like Jacob's coat of many colors. It takes a strong man in these times, though, to stand up to the rack when there isn't much in it but ammunition, and it's grimly give and take with no white feather mix, and neither army will give up. Wonder if we won't be abused for all this bye and bye by other than copperheads?

M<small>ONDAY</small>, Sept. 12, 1864.

We are having a nice long time in camp, but will probably make up for it when Grant and Sheridan get this little army fixed to suit them. I have been in fights thus far with Companies B, D, and K, having commanded the two latter in a number of hot places, and now I am First Lieutenant Commanding Company

E. I don't stay with a Company long enough to learn all the men's names, but they impress me with the idea that they are not dissatisfied with me even if I only know them by sight. Company B is from Barre, Montpelier and Waterbury. D from Burlington, E from Bennington, and K from Derby Line, and the men are *splendid* fighters, at any rate with me. I don't try to drive them into a fight but am lucky to keep up with the intrepid leaders and most of the rest follow. Except the bravest of them, the others are not apt to go where their Commander won't, and I get better work out of them by keeping ahead of them if I only can. Some of them are so dauntlessly courageous they inspire me.

Tuesday, Sept. 13, 1864.

Well, the papers begin to speak encouragingly, and reinforcements are rapidly being sent Grant and Thomas. We have got but few yet, but rumor says that six hundred left Vermont on the seventh of September for our regiment. It's cloudy and there's a chilly south wind. It threatens rain. McClellan's party is demanding a new candidate. Well, let it have one, it will be all the better for Mr. Lincoln. All's quiet to-night.

Wednesday, Sept. 14, 1864.

Rather a gloomy day. It rained hard from 9 o'clock a. m. until about noon. Lieutenants Davis, Welch and Wheeler have gone on picket with a hundred men from our regiment. There was Company drill this afternoon. It rained so this forenoon that battalion drill was suspended; rained hard this evening, too. Election returns from Maine this evening show that State to be strongly Republican.

Thursday, Sept. 15, 1864.

It was fair until 5 o'clock p. m. when it sprinkled slightly and prevented dress parade. We had battalion drill this forenoon and Company drill this afternoon. The Commissary came up this forenoon, too, with rations. We have received a large mail. All well at home. The Second Division of the Sixth Corps and a brigade of cavalry made a reconnoissance to-day toward Opequan Creek where the Vermont Brigade skirmishers located the enemy just beyond Opequan Creek with its line facing east, its right flank resting on the Berryville pike and its left on the Martinsburg pike with Winchester in its rear. Our armies are about six miles apart.

Friday, Sept. 16, 1864.

It's a delightful evening; has been pleasant all day. There was battalion and company drill this forenoon and afternoon respectively. Extracts from the Richmond Examiner and other Southern journals state that Lee's army about

Richmond is in terrible condition, is living on half rations, clothes worn out and no prospect of getting more. It has got so they have to use negroes to transport supplies, etc. I wouldn't blame that army for changing its politics or anything else to get out of the scrape it's in.

SATURDAY, Sept. 17, 1864.

Warm and pleasant: gentle south breeze; looks like a southern storm. General Grant came to-day, but has gone. It looks like a move. Fifty men from our regiment went on picket this afternoon. We have been moving camp, another indication of a move. Let it come. Orry Blanchard and Nate Harrington have been over this evening.

SUNDAY, Sept. 18, 1864.

It's cloudy with a gentle south breeze. We had company inspection at 9 o'clock this forenoon and monthly at 4 o'clock this afternoon. The supply train came at 8 o'clock a. m. with four days' rations. We got orders at 3 o'clock p. m. to strike tents which we did, and march at once, but the order was countermanded. We shall probably move early in the morning. There's a high south wind this evening, but it doesn't look like rain. Sheridan's army now consists of three infantry corps, three divisions of cavalry and the usual complement of artillery, in all about 30,000 men, as follows; The Sixth Corps, Major General H. G. Wright, U. S. V. commanding; the Eighth Corps, Major-General George Crook, U. S. V. commanding; the Nineteenth Corps, Brevet Major-General W. H. Emery commanding; Brevet Major-General A. T. A. Torbert, U. S. V., Chief of Cavalry; the First Division of Cavalry, Brigadier-General Wesley Merritt, U. S. V. commanding; the Second Division of Cavalry, Brigadier-General W. W. Averell, U. S. A. commanding; and of the Third Division of Cavalry, Brigadier-General James H. Wilson, U. S. V. commanding. Lieutenant-General Jubal A. Early commands the Confederate army with about the same force.

MONDAY, Sept. 19, 1864.

We received orders at 10 o'clock last night to march at 2 o'clock this morning which we did. Daylight brought us up near Opequan Creek on the Winchester-Berryville pike. Wilson's Cavalry had charged and carried the enemy's picket line and earthworks protecting the pike near both the East and West entrance of the gorge through which this road runs, taken a goodly number of prisoners, and it looked like business again. A large number of troops moved in two or more columns across the Opequan for about a mile and then up the narrow winding pike in one column through a little valley or gorge, known as the Berryville canyon to us, but as Ash Hollow locally, with second growth or scrub oak and ash trees and underbrush coming close down its scraggy abrupt banks two hundred feet high more or less in places after crossing Abraham Creek, to the road and rivulet winding along the gorge for nearly three miles—the source of which stream is wrongly given on all maps pertaining to this battle—on past General Sheridan near the west end of the canyon towards Winchester sitting on his horse a little off the road to the right in the open field on slightly ascending ground watching the column our brigade was in which, owing to its plucky fight under great disadvantages at the Battle of the Monocacy which largely saved the city of Washington barely nine weeks before, he had selected for the most important point in his line of battle at the head of the gorge on the pike to Winchester with our valiant regiment and the Fourteenth New Jersey planted across it even the colors of each which were in the centre of the regiments, being in the center of the pike and the rest of the army ordered to guide on us. *Surely* this *was* the place of honor in the battle that day for the Sixth Corps followed the pike in all the assaults of the day which was quite crooked including the first one until the enemy was driven completely routed through the city of Winchester when night put an end to the fighting Sheridan restlessly urged the men across a small ravine opposite where he sat, his eyes wandering occasionally everywhere over the large open space which gradually rose to the vast comparatively level but slightly rolling battlefield in our front, as the men looked curiously at him so near I could touch him as we marched, little dreaming that three years after I should be honored for my work that day, which he saw, by being a member of his staff, or that he would be instrumental in saving my life when ill with malignant yellow fever and threatened with fatal black vomit in New Orleans, La. in 1867, by sending his cook, a faithful old colored woman, who was an expert nurse of yellow fever patients, to care for me. It was the nearest we had ever been to him, and as our regiment passed slowly by fours, the line being congested ahead, the men took a good look at him for he was already famous and every soldier's ideal hero; and as they did so they unconsciously slackened their sauntering pace a little which was what caused Sheridan to urge them on.

We were on the eve of the most brilliant spectacular battle of the war, at any rate that I had seen, and my ideal genius developed by the great Civil War—Sheridan was to lead us; and the valor of the renowned Sixth Corps, his pet of all the splendid corps of as grand and valiant an army as ever existed—the Army of the Potomac—was about being placed by him at the most important point in line of battle ready to do and die for him, the Vermont troops or "Green Mountain Boys," as we were called through every city we passed, and especially our regiment being one of two to occupy the keystone position or place of honor on the famous historic Berryville and Winchester pike in the great assaulting line on a battlefield slightly rolling but level in places as a house floor when once fairly on it, to take another stitch out of rebellion, and to help immortalize our hero, and we did both. Aye! we shall glorify Sheridan continually as a military genius, even as he has honored us as his ideal soldiers and fighters heretofore, now and probably will evermore, the grand old Sixth Army Corps which fights everything everywhere, and rarely gives up fighting till called off, but, alas! which will soon only be a hallowed, glorified memory; and—still—I like to think of it in reflective moments as in a celebrated painting of a bivouacked army at night asleep watched over by an army of hovering angels in midair; that it as a hallowed spiritual body finally at peace in a heavenly paradise, will go marching on throughout the boundless everlasting realms of eternity ever to hover approvingly when occasion shall require over other mortal armies of dauntless valor and constancy such as it has been in the great Civil War—*one of God's instruments for the betterment of humanity and civil liberty*—the most admired, honored, trusted and beloved by military geniuses of its period.

After passing Sheridan about two hundred yards we arrived at the height of the land westerly from Opequan Creek where the Sixth and Nineteenth Corps were finally formed in lines of battle running about North and South behind a narrow belt of timber, except a little in front of the reserve, facing nearly west toward Winchester about two miles away. The formation of the ground at this point occupied by the Tenth Vermont and Second Brigade was unusually peculiar. The turnpike from this place virtually runs along the divide westerly towards Winchester between the nameless Creek we came up after crossing the Opequan and Abraham Creek, now on our right and north and the latter on our left to the south for a goodly distance the reason for which is obvious as in all such cases where streams have abrupt banks, while at the point where we debouched from the gulch we came up and formed line of battle was another little divide running north and south the east slope of which is partially an easterly watershed for Opequan Creek, and the west slope for the ravine or nameless rivulet running south about two hundred and fifty yards in front of where we first formed line of battle in which was the enemy's infantry in strong force—probably two divisions or more—in front of our Third Division but not shown on any map of this battlefield I have ever seen, not even the official government one used in Haynes' "History of the Tenth Vermont Volunteer Infantry." (See No. 3, 6, 7 and 8 illustrations). It is the ravine through which the little short rivulet runs shown on said map just in front of our "First position" running southerly into a tributary of Abraham Creek. I am *emphatic* in this statement as having been on the battlefield twice since the fight occurred within a year (1908) for the purpose of trying to correct false history and maps, I know whereof I write. I desire to impress this on all historians for I know of no one living who, owing to my elevated advanced position on the battlefield knows more of it. These two small divides before mentioned meet each other at right angles forming a letter T. The pike crosses the horizontal part of the T on leaving the gulch we came up from the

Opequan in, and virtually runs along the first mentioned divide slightly to the left of all rivulet sources running southerly, forming the perpendicular part of the T towards Winchester.

About a half mile to the right or north of the pike and about two hundred and fifty yards in front of our line of battle before advancing, a little to my right, the rivulet before mentioned, where the enemy was, heads, running in a partial semicircle the slightly convex side towards the right half of the Tenth Vermont and the concave side caused by a bend in the rivulet virtually at its source was largely in front of the Second brigade; (See No. 8 illustration) the stream runs southerly and drops rapidly after crossing the pike thus forming a gulch similar to the one we came up from the Opequan in, but apparently deeper and narrower near the left front of the Second Division. This sudden drop to the left of the turnpike made the divide here running north and south quite decided being fully ninety feet high or more which will probably partly account for the enemy's mostly being to the right of the pike there being no protection immediately west from the divide running North and South. In my front on the right of the pike this divide was about fifty feet high running out rapidly on to almost level ground in front of the right of the Second Brigade of our division to my right, which made its position untenable as the ground was swept by both the enemy's artillery and infantry.

The formation in front of the Nineteenth Corps which was our infantry right in the noon or first assault of the day was entirely different. (See Nos. 4 and 5 illustrations). Its whole front after about three hundred yards down a gentle slope was broad and comparatively level with slight breaks several hundred yards across, but not probably impassable for infantry at any point, where three or more small rivulets apparently headed with banks so undefined and flat as to give no defensive protection in a military sense so the enemy had no men or infantry there so far as I could see, but did have at least a small showing of artillery which I could see far across the breaks. These rivulets run northerly probably into the rivulet we came up from the Opequan or the Red Bud, but I do not know this. They help to form a morass it is said, probably about a mile more or less from where I was about fifty feet wide in front of where Crook's Corps was later in the day and it was probably here that Colonel R. B. Hayes (Nineteenth President, U. S. A.) later in the day, at the head of his brigade plunged in on his horse which at once mired when he dismounted and waded across alone under fire followed as soon as he waved his hat to them to join him, by about forty of his men to try and capture a battery which, led by him, they did after a hand-to-hand fight with the gunners, the enemy having deemed the battery so secure that no infantry support had been placed near it,which indicates that in this assault the bulk of the enemy's infantry force confronting our infantry was at first largely in front of our division on the pike. The trees in number 4 illustration along the breaks in 1864 were not there then. The open foreground is the divide running east and west in this illustration so it can be easily seen why the Nineteenth Corps had no considerable fighting to do here.

The left of the enemy's line of infantry in the ravine in my front, so far as I could see, ended about nine hundred yards to my right at the head of the ravine as there was no cover further north except beyond the divide running east and west a good distance away to the north in front of the Nineteenth Corps, and its line was bent to conform to the ravine's direction in my right front; (See No. 8 illustration) the head of the rivulet had quite flat banks the convex side of the creek and its near and most abrupt bank being toward us in my front, but the reverse at the head of the ravine. This was the point in the enemy's line where the gap in our lines occurred mentioned further on which owing to the flat artillery and musketry-swept ground was untenable for the Second Brigade or any force except large enough to drive the enemy's infantry from its cover as was Russell's. (See Nos. 4 and 5 illustrations). If the historian hereafter accuses the Third Division of breaking in this assault, it will be but fair to state extenuating circumstances, for a portion of the First Brigade was similarly situated and we got no direct effective flank help from our critics on either flank during the fight. The pike from our line of battle ran in an *air line about nine hundred yards directly towards Winchester* (See Nos. 2 and 9 illustrations) and was practically level except where it crossed the divide and little rivulet near my front where in the ravine the enemy had such a strong force in front of us about a regiment of which moved there across the pike from in front of the left of our First Brigade, (See No. 6 illustration) the Second Division having nothing in its immediate front in the ravine and the Vermont Brigade only a weak force in its distant left front beyond, but what a regiment could probably have easily handled and probably less than that did; but, nevertheless, that part of the Second Division next to us obliqued to the left to attack it which was what caused that Division to pull away from the Third Division's left at the same time the Nineteenth Corps pulled away from our right causing wide gaps—as the position which should have been occupied by the Second Brigade was vacant, too—thus leaving our brigade and especially our regiment, alone at a critical time when the gallant General Russell with his magnificent Division so grandly marched in and filled the gap on my right and lost his life in the act. (See No. 5 illustration). Our colors were on the pike thus bringing the right half of our regiment to the north or right side of it on open ground (See Nos. 3 and 5 illustrations) and leaving only about three regiments of our Division to the left of it on the wooded side hill (as shown in Nos. 3 and 7 illustrations) soon sloping abruptly towards the ravine in front which gave all our troops to the left of our colors on the pike some welcome cover but the right of our regiment and the Second Brigade, none. (See Nos. 3, 4, 5 and 6 illustrations).

The distance locally from where we crossed the Opequan to Winchester is called five miles; and to where we formed line of battle three miles, and from thence to Winchester two miles. The local distance from Winchester to Stephenson's Station by the railroad is six miles and to Summit Station twelve miles. There is no map in existence known to me giving the correct position of the enemy's infantry in the ravine in front of the Third Division, Sixth Corps; it is placed nearly a half mile too far back or west, and nearer where the second assault of the day was. The illustrations which of course must be correct herein place the enemy right in front of the Third Division and I can make oath to it, in the first assault when I was twice wounded. But I will now return a little and endeavor to describe this brilliant battle.

We were drawn up as before stated, in two lines of battle at the west entrance of the canyon facing west on an open field about midway between Abraham Creek on the south and Red Bud Creek on the north just in rear of a long narrow strip of woods which served as a great curtain to a grand, broad, slightly rolling plain several miles in extent in every direction in our front, which was to be the stage that day with the city of Winchester in the background, of one of the most dashing, picturesque battles probably ever fought in ancient or modern times at first with beautiful, silent nature about the only witness. The Third Division, Sixth Corps, was in the left and most important center of the line in two lines, the Tenth Vermont on the Berryville-Winchester pike, the most important, dangerous and stubbornly contested point in the whole line; the Nineteenth Corps was on our right in two lines; the intrepid Second Division, Sixth Corps in which was the gallant First Vermont Brigade, was on our left, one of the easiest places in the line; General Russell's valiant First Division, Sixth Corps, as reserve was stationed en masse a short distance in rear of where the right flank of the Third Division, Sixth Corps, and the left flank of the Nineteenth Corps joined, which was within a short distance and in plain sight of where I was, and our three Divisions of dashing, picturesque cavalry—including Wilson on our left along Abraham Creek running south of Winchester and Senseny Road, and Merritt and Averill on our right along the railroad and the Martinsburg pike—was massed on either flank for assault at the right moment on the enemy's flanks or as occasion might demand, while Crook's Eighth Corps was about a quarter of a mile en masse about in rear of the right flank of the Nineteenth Corps.

At noon in the midst of a perfect bedlam caused by the roar of artillery, shrieking, bursting, hurtling shells, and the voices of many officers pitched high so as to be heard above the din, giving orders, the assault was made through the thin strip of timber in our front toward Winchester when we briefly halted and laid on the ground, and then across an open field beyond the woods in all about two hundred and fifty yards where I was, midst a perfect storm of solid shot and shell, rattling musketry on my right and front, and whizzing minie balls without being able to fire a rifle at first so well was the enemy in my front protected by the lay of the ground and its rail breast-works. We persistently advanced, though, but it took a great deal of nerve and will power to do it in an open field without the slightest cover, all the time midst a perfect storm of iron and leaden hail and the cries of the wounded and dying which were disconcerting, until we drove the enemy back pell mell from its works in my front in the utmost confusion—yes, in a perfect stampede for they were old soldiers and knew when they were whipped, and when it was necessary to run with all their might to save themselves from slaughter and ignominious capture. (See Nos. 3 foreground and Nos. 5 and 6 illustrations).

The Tenth Vermont, Fourteenth New Jersey and the rest of our brigade as usual, not only proudly led the Division at first by a good deal in the advance through the woods but in this instance the whole army. It was therefore not only the most aggressive and conspicuous part of—being on high ground where I could see our line of battle each way—but the most important point in the line; was first seen when through the wood and the most dreaded by the enemy being on the pike, and in consequence its artillery fire within reach was concentrated on us, *and it was a hot place.* But soon, after recovering from the collapse of the Second Brigade on my right which wholly disappeared and nothing more was seen of it by me, with the valor of the old-time "Green Mountain Boys" on we went undaunted until, after we had advanced about seventy-five yards beyond the woods now extinct behind which we had formed in the open field where I was, being then on a high point where I could see the whole battlefield, I glanced to my right and left and was appalled to see that the troops on both flanks of my Brigade were obliquing rapidly away from us, the whole Nineteenth Corps in perfect lines of battle by an oblique movement to the right having pulled away from the right of our Division until there was a gap big enough including that made by the Second Brigade, to more than admit a Brigade line of battle although it is said that Corps had been directed to guide on our Division and that a similar state of affairs existed on our left flank where the Vermont brigade was. (See No. 3 through opening in woods showing No. 7; also see No. 5 where I was in the foreground). With a feeling of dismay I slackened my pace and nearly halted for I saw that through the gap in the very center and most vital point in our line on my right towards the Nineteenth Corps opposite which point was a strong force of the enemy's infantry awaiting us behind its works on the near edge of a little valley which protected it from our fire until right on it, it would throw its force so situated opposite the gap on our right and left flanks caused by the gap and have us completely at its mercy; but glancing almost immediately again to my right and rear, hearing loud military commands there, my spirits rose as I saw the gallant Russell leading his splendid Division en masse through the opening in the timber in his front, magnificently forward as though at drill to fill the gap. The appearance of his column greatly relieved us, as it drew the concentrated artillery fire from our column by the enemy largely to his. The whole battle scene at this moment at this point was one of appalling grandeur, one which no beholders could ever forget, provided they could keep their nerve well enough to preserve their presence of mind sufficiently to take in the situation midst the screeching shells and appalling musketry fire. The splendid appearance of General Russell's Division elicited a cry of admiration from all who saw it. It was the supreme moment or turning point in the great tide of battle, and as Russell's men rapidly deployed latterly under a galling fire on the march either way in perfect order enough to fill the gap, it was magnificent—beyond description—the grandest, best and most welcome sight I ever saw in a tight place in battle, and so inspired me—seeing the danger of a flank movement had passed—I again pushed forward to be in front and was there when the intrepid General Russell, one of the best fighters in the army, was twice shot and soon died a short distance to my right rear just about the time I was also twice hit; (see Nos. 5 and 6 illustrations) but when the enemy in my front and all along the little valley caught sight of our reserve coming at them so majestically and in such solid phalanx and splendid order, it seemed to me the rebs couldn't run fast enough apparently to get away. It was the most sudden transformation on a battlefield I ever saw, as well as the most perfect stampede and rout; and it was the enemy's last volley when it saw our reserve coming at them so determinedly that put a stop to my fighting for several months; and but for our reserve coming on the field just as it did I would have been worse riddled than I was by the enemy and killed even lying on the ground wounded, as I was wholly exposed where I lay close on their works not a rod away, the ground sloping towards them.

General Sheridan's plan of battle was perfect and I shall never cease to admire him as the greatest military genius I have ever seen on a battlefield, for by this and his pluck and dash, I see the secret of his great successes. The plan of battle was fully developed by the time I fell twice badly wounded—at first I supposed mortally—only a few feet in front of the enemy's works, and as I arose partially recovered from the shock of being twice hit, quivering and bleeding profusely, one of the first things my eye caught was Sheridan all alone without a staff officer or even an orderly near him, about forty yards in my rear, sitting his splendid thoroughbred horse like a centaur looking—all animation his very pose suggesting it—intently through his field glass toward the fleeing routed enemy and later after the third and last assault of the day all in a jumble with our undaunted dashing cavalry in perfect order sweeping across the great comparatively level plain bordering Winchester, like a tornado, with banners, arms, brasses, etc., brightly gleaming in the blazing autumn sunlight—a battle scene, as badly as I was wounded, the forepart of which held me entranced. As I again soon turned after the first assault, Sheridan put spurs to his horse and off he dashed all animation to another part of the field to reform his line and so on, going finally like the wind into the very midst of the great congested jumble, the enemy trying like a frightened flock of sheep to force itself through the streets of Winchester all at one time, the men literally piling themselves at the main street entrances on top of each other in order to do so. No battle scene will remain photographed so vividly on my memory as the first part of this for I could see nearly the whole field from where I long remained.

The fatal wounding in my sight near enough to hear his cry of anguish of my old Captain—Major Dillingham—and the killing of Major Vredenburg of the Fourteenth New Jersey from his horse by having his heart torn out, and others; General Russell's brilliant debouch with his dauntless division marching proudly on the battlefield en masse with all its enchanting glitter and precision to take a hand at the sacrifice of his life—unfortunate, gallant, dashing Russell —Merritt, Averill and Custer's brilliant spirited final charges on the fleeing enemy, its disorder and worst possible rout all beggar description, our retreat at the battle of Monocacy, July 9, 1864, being one of order and dignity comparatively speaking. I felt revenged for my wound and at having to run so in retreat at the Monocacy, and for my two wounds that day even if I did totteringly tarry, maimed and speechless with paralyzed tongue, chin and blanched face to look at such a brilliant battle scene until I became so faint from loss of blood, shock and partial reaction, I could hardly go steadily and finally did accept help, having declined at first, from two faithful men of my Company who, when I fell instead of stampeding stayed by me in one of the hottest places I have ever been in on a battlefield, one of whom was Corporal Joel Walker of Pownal, Vt. My first wound was from the butt end of an exploding shell in the breast which maimed and knocked me down and simultaneously as I fell a minie ball fired but a rod away in my front just grazed my forehead, torn through my upper lip crushing both jaws and carrying away eleven teeth, the most painless dentistry I ever had done; but, Oh! the shock it gave my system and the misery I suffered that night!

As I entered the long broad avenue running between the great tents at the field hospital later in the day where there were hundreds of wounded, dead and dying, Dillingham, Hill and others of my regiment, among the number, Dr. J. C. Rutherford, one of my regimental surgeons, seeing me with a man on either side—for here in sight of others I wouldn't let them support me—close to and keenly watching my unsteady carriage, came running, hastily examined my wounds, bade me sit on the ground, ran for his instrument case, placed my head upturned between his knees, sewed in place a triangular piece of flesh extending from the right corner of my nose down hanging at the lower right corner by a slight shred of flesh, which I had held in place from the battlefield with my fingers, and that job for the time being was done; but oh! my aching head, jaws and chest, as well as the extreme feeling of lassitude for the balance of the day. My face was like a puff ball, so quickly had it swollen, my chest at the point of the wishbone—so to speak—was mangled black and blue and resembled a pounded piece of steak ready to be cooked, and I was so nauseated, lame and sore all over, I dreaded to move. I guess the rebs came pretty near winging me—but Glory! Early was licked. To add to my feeling of depression, I was told Major Dillingham was mortally wounded and that he would soon pass away. He had been a good friend, a brave man, faultlessly courageous, was an elegant gentleman and good fellow, and was much beloved. A solid shot severed a leg going through the woods; his cry of anguish was distressing, and I shrink from thinking of it whenever it comes into my mind.

I fell just in front of the enemy's hastily thrown up breastworks of fence rails in the vanguard after advancing under a murderous fire about a hundred yards or more, in the open field after passing through the woods. I saw no other line officer with his men anywhere in my vicinity so far in front, and there was no other officer there in the open field except Adjutant Wyllys Lyman who was lauded for it, but I, being a boy, got nothing but my two wounds as compliments for my steadfastness, and they will stay with me through life. I wonder if when across the Great River and in another world I will be remembered any better for my faithfulness when so many others failed at such an important moment?

I found the men of Company E good fighters, Corporal Walker and another big man of my Company whose name I can't recall, being so short a time with the Company—but believe it was one of the Brownells, also of Pownal, Vt.—who helped me occasionally going to the ambulance as I felt faint and weak, were brave fellows. They followed me closely all through the assault as though they expected me to be hit, fighting like heroes as they were at the same time, and when I fell wounded they dropped close by me, Corporal Walker, a giant, coolly saying: "Don't get up Lieutenant, they'll riddle you if you do!" but I thought they already had. However, the nervous shock of both wounds was too great to think of rising at once, and almost immediately the rebs were running for dear life all branches of the service mixed together in confusion—a perfect jumble. We had licked them in a square stand up open field fight of their own choice—and a very poor one, too, for them in case of defeat, as it proved—and it was clean cut, the worst stampede and rout I ever saw.

Sheridan was as brave as a lion, and unlike some commanders who hunt cover when their commands are fighting, went seemingly fearlessly anywhere he wanted to in order to see what was going on and what if any part of the line needed reinforcing. As before stated, my position on the battlefield was sufficiently high to see nearly all of it. It being a beautiful sunny Fall day with a clear atmosphere, it was the most spectacular, and before the Infantry broke, the most beautiful battlefield sight seen, and better yet, the most snappy, brilliant fighting witnessed during the war. Sheridan hovered near the centre in the neighborhood of the high ground where I was twice wounded, and dashed back and forth the line on horseback like a restless lion, an ideally alert fighter, almost as unmindful of shot and shell as though both deaf and blind. It was here that I formed my opinion that he was not only the ideal fighter, but the second, if not the greatest military genius developed by the Civil War, and I have never changed my opinion. Honest, alert, aggressive, dashing and brave with splendid judgment, his equal will be hard to find, and probably rarely surpassed. He was generally conceded a brilliant cavalry fighter, but if the world has ever produced a better planned, executed, dashing, brilliant, spectacular, snappy battle or commander than he and this Battle of Winchester, where the different branches of the service were combined, take it from first to last during the day, it would be interesting to know on what occasion. It was so unlike any battle ever seen by me that all others sink into insignificance as dull affairs. Language or words even with the most gifted talkers or writers can never describe this battle; no pen picture, or ever so gifted talker can do it justice; it would have to be seen by an expert to be fully appreciated. Ever afterwards the Sixth Corps of all others was Sheridan's favorite. Said he later: "Give me the Sixth Corps and I will charge anywhere."

Among the most admirable pictures of the fight—barring the orderly, majestic advance to battle of the whole army in unbroken lines—except after a little our division being unmercifully shelled from the start on the pike it could not withstand it, nor could any other have done so—as a whole after through the wood resembling an immense gracefully waving blue ribbon along the surface of the ground, caused by that enchantingly swinging, billowy motion characteristic of regulars when marching in large bodies, its fluttering banners, glittering arms, equipments and its blue uniforms looking prettier than ever in the bright September sunlight under a bright blue sky specked with fleecy white clouds making a picture beautiful with perfect harmony of color,—was the beauty, grandeur and majesty of both Russell and Custer's splendid debouch on the battlefield with their valiant, intrepid commands, the former's proudly and majestically en masse in perfect order and cadence, line and bearing, coolly confident as though at parade, and the latter's also in perfect lines and order, as well as dashing, intrepid, spirited and assured bearing even the horses as though vieing with each other in speed to run down the unfortunate enemy, entering into the spirit of the occasion and sweeping rapidly like an avalanche down on the demoralized, fleeing and awe-stricken enemy with the fury and apparently almost certain destruction of a tornado. These were pictures comprising awe, beauty, power, grandeur, order and disorder, dash, magnificence, valor, terror, confusion, inspiration and majesty to such an extent as to defy the pen picture of any writer however gifted. This battle was different from any other I ever saw. It was Sheridan's way of doing things—a revelation in warfare.

So far as this first assault is concerned it can be summed up quite briefly. The only considerable amount of the enemy's infantry in the *immediate* front of the Union infantry line of battle was in the ravine in front of our division, and it was about two hundred and fifty yards away from where we formed line behind the woods; it was a very strong force. If the troops to our right and left instead of instinctively obliquing away from us veteran like to an easier place in their right and left fronts respectively, had guided on our division as it is claimed they were directed to do, they would have had an enfilading fire on the enemy on our front, the same as General Russell's division would have had when it filled the gap to my right which the enemy knew would make their position untenable and so instantaneously retreated in a rout when it saw him coming dangerously near, his right flank overlapping their left. When Russell's movement was executed the Nineteenth Corps' lines of battle hadn't even broken. There was no considerable number of the enemy before it within striking distance so far as I could see, and therefore *nothing* to break its lines so far as the enemy was concerned until it reached the breaks in its front.

The Vermont Brigade could have easily advanced at any time of the assault or any other part of the Second Division, as there was nothing to speak of—as virtually acknowledged by Colonel Aldace F. Walker of that brigade in his "History of the Vermont Brigade in the Shenandoah Valley, 1864"—in its immediate front except about a regiment of the enemy which crossed the pike from his right and the left of our Brigade to my front. (See No. 7 illustration). Had the Vermont Brigade borne to its right instead of its left it would have done much more effective service, as it would have been on high ground overlooking the enemy in my front when out of the ravine. In this instance the credit given this excellent brigade in at least one Civil War history is erroneous, without the Third Division was expected to whip *at once* and alone a considerable part of the infantry and artillery of Early's army in its immediate front, no small part of which was in our regimental front and its immediate right. In proof that there was no considerable rebel force in front of the Second Division to the *left* of the pike until Early's second stand, the reader is invited to examine the official War Department map of this battle and note the fact; but aside from this I *know* there was none. What, therefore, was to prevent the Second Division or Vermont Brigade from advancing? Unlike our front, where the strip of timber was narrow, with the enemy strongly posted just beyond, the scrub or second growth oak, etc., in front of a part of the Second Division next to us, extended from the top of the ridge or divide which ran several hundred yards southerly, down to the bottom of the ravine a hundred yards more or less, which covered here the Second Division's advance and the cleared ground beyond, after emerging from the wooded side hill and ravine towards Winchester, contained no force of the enemy, as there was no immediate protection for it, sufficient to prevent its or even the Vermont Brigade's advancing, or the enemy would have done so. (See Nos. 3, 7 and 8 illustrations.) I mention this here because I *know* the facts in the premises, and because this Division is complimented—unfortunately, but probably unwittingly so—in one or more histories for advancing, in unpleasant contrast to our Division, which was up against the*real* thing, and its advancing depended largely on the help or enfilading fire along our front, we had a right to expect from the troops which should have guided on us from both flanks, but which we never got, as they pulled away from us. It was useless to try to take such a place as confronted the right of our regiment and Division by assaulting from its immediate front (see Nos. 5 and 6 illustrations), as the enemy had to be flanked out of its position, which is what Russell's men would have done on the rebel left in case the enemy hadn't seen them in season to get away and thereby saved many casualties on both sides, and probably largely there the enemy's capture.

There were none of the Second Brigade of our Division on my right after advancing through the woods, nor had there been up to the time General Russell's command filled the gap occasioned by the Second Brigade's absence, together with the space caused by the Nineteenth Corps obliquing to its right. It being level, shell and bullet swept, it was untenable until a force came large enough to drive the enemy's infantry from cover, as Russell did. (See No. 5 illustration). I was the only officer except Adjutant Wyllys Lyman, who is deceased, so far ahead at that time on my part of the battlefield, and I can make affidavit to this statement. We and a goodly number of scattering men who generally led in most assaults were within a rod of the enemy's *strongest* manned works, *which no map in existence shows* that I have seen, where I was twice almost instantaneously wounded when the enemy ran as it saw General Russell's Division coming, as though their lives depended upon it, and I *know*whereof I am writing.

General Sheridan made no mistake when he selected the First Brigade for the centre and most important point of his line of battle, nor was it a mistake to place our regiment and the Fourteenth New Jersey—with direction for the rest of the army to guide on our Division in the first assault, for the road was practically straight—squarely across the pike, with their colors on it, with such men as Corporals Alexander Scott, F. H. Hoadley, Tenth Vermont, and other of the color guard like them, to keep them there, for such men would go wherever told to, if into the very jaws of death. The leaving off from the official map of this battle of the enemy's infantry in the ravine in front of the Third Division (see Nos. 6 and 8 illustrations), is a great injustice to our regiment, which never wholly fell back, but the usual per cent. of men under such circumstances stubbornly pressed forward under the most trying circumstances at any rate where I was. The leaving off of the enemy's infantry in my front, where it was strongest, is misleading and is doubtless what has caused so many wrong descriptions of this fight. No one can give a correct description of it where I was except at that point during the fight. The enemy contested this point more stubbornly than any other during the day and it was here the most intrepid of our men assaulted; it was the doorway to the great battlefield, and if the enemy couldn't hold this point it couldn't hope to any other, and didn't. Although our division was smaller than either of the other divisions of our Corps, its loss was much heavier. General Grant had one hundred shotted guns fired on his lines in front of Petersburg in honor of this day's victory by Sheridan. A citizen of Winchester told me that one of the saddest things he saw during the day was a horse going through the streets of the city with two badly wounded and one dead Confederate soldiers on it— probably chums—the latter thrown over the horse's back with his head and arms hanging on one side and his feet on the other; but war is a cruel teacher and produces the most shocking sights imaginable. It is not pleasant to record and much less dwell on them.

The following pertaining to Sheridan's battle of Winchester has been discovered since writing the foregoing. It will be answered in detail. Says Col. Aldace F. Walker in his "History of the Vermont Brigade in the Shenandoah Valley, 1864," pp. 91-100:

"Our movement commenced at 3 o'clock Monday morning, September 19th, Getty's Division having the advance, the Vermont Brigade being the last in the Division. Striking directly across the country, at first in the darkness, we presently reached the main road from Berryville to Winchester, and moved down it to the crossing of the Opequan. This stream is considerably below the level of the adjoining country, and the road on its further side keeps the low level of the stream for a mile or more, winding through a long, tortuous wooded ravine, our unobstructed passage whereof was for the time a mystery. It seems that Wilson's Division of cavalry had already cleared the way and was then holding desperately a position that it had gained with considerable loss, but which proved a most admirable one in which to deploy our line of battle.

"As we filed out of the ravine which toward the last was lined with wounded cavalrymen, we found Sheridan, his headquarters fixed on a conspicuous elevation, personally superintending from the commencement the operations of the day. It was to be our first battle under his command, as well as his first independent battle; the troops were hitherto destitute of all enthusiasm for him; fortunately, however, no impression save a favorable one had as yet been received, it being universally conceded that he had so far handled his army handsomely. And it was with great satisfaction that we found him in this early twilight at the very front, and under the fire of the enemy, carefully attending to details which we had been accustomed to see more celebrated commanders entrust to their staff.

"Our Division promptly relieved the cavalry and formed its line facing west, the Third Brigade which was in advance going to what was to be the extreme left of the infantry line, resting on Abraham Creek; the First Brigade following, took up its position on the right of the Third, and our own Brigade filled the remaining distance between the First and the road on which we had reached the battlefield. It had been intended to place us in two lines, but the unexpected extent of the ground we had to cover forbade that formation. We were just on the hither edge of a narrow fringe of wood that concealed us from the enemy; the Sixth Vermont was thrown forward as a skirmish line perhaps one hundred yards to the further side of the little forest, and at once engaged the enemy's skirmishers."

About three regiments, I believe, of the First Brigade, Third Division, Sixth Corps, were to the left or south of the road, so the Vermont Brigade didn't reach to the pike.

"Near us in the road at our right was a rebel field work, taken by Wilson in the night. The hill on which it was situated commanded the country in both directions, and it was already occupied by a battery engaged in feeling the enemy, which was answered vigorously, many of the rebel shell plunging over into the troops as they successively came up the road.

"Our Division thus formed in a single line was the only Division on the south or left of the road. The Third Division, Ricketts', followed us and prolonged the line across and on the north of the road, placing its two Brigades in two lines. The First Division, Russell's, came next, and was drawn up behind the Third as a third line or reserve, also somewhat overlapping the right of our Brigade."

About three regiments or more of the Third Division, Sixth Corps, I believe, were south of the road, on the right of the Second Division. When General Russell's Division charged it was about two hundred yards to the right of the Tenth Vermont, or about seven hundred yards or more to the right of Col. Walker's brigade.

"Then to our surprise no more troops appeared, and our Corps was alone confronting the enemy. There were two or three anxious hours, but Early was engaged in hurrying up his detachment from Bunker Hill, which this delay gave him ample time to do, and made no assault. It was said that the Nineteenth Corps, being ordered to follow the Sixth, had filed into the road behind our wagon train, instead of keeping closed up on our column. It is certain that with this loss of time, from whatever reason it occurred, we lost the opportunity of attacking the enemy in detail, and gave him time to prepare for our reception. It was noon before the Nineteenth Corps had reached its place and was formed in three or four lines on the right of the Sixth."

The Nineteenth Corps was formed in two lines on the right of the Sixth.

"Our men during the forenoon had been resting, sitting or lying on the ground. When at last the disposition was completed and the signal gun was fired, they sprang to the ranks, and the line advanced. Particular instructions had been received to the effect that the road was to give the direction of attack, and that the guiding regiment was to be the left regiment of the Third Division, just across the road from our right."

The guiding regiments were the Tenth Vermont and Fourteenth New Jersey, on the right of the First Brigade, about the center of the Third Division.

"In passing through the bit of trees in our front, which was filled with underbrush, our line was necessarily thrown somewhat into confusion. When we emerged from the wood and the ground over which we must make our attack was developed, the prospect was appalling. The hill gradually sloped away before us, for a quarter of a mile, to a long ravine, irregular in its course, but its windings extending either way as far as we could see. The ascent beyond it was in most places sharp, and the enemy held its crest in force, perfectly commanding with musketry and artillery the long slope down which we must pass, though the acclivity on the further side of the hollow was so steep as to actually present a cover from their fire—if it could once be reached.

"When this fearful prospect opened the line involuntarily halted, and the men threw themselves on the ground as was their wont when under fire. Our own Brigade was properly waiting for the movement of the guiding regiment which lay across the road a little to our rear, and which could not be prevailed upon to stir. To add to the peril of the situation, the road, instead of continuing straight on, as seems to have been expected, here made a bend to the left so that our original orders could not be obeyed without an amount of obliquing that would have resulted in demoralization; from this cause our own Brigade was soon afterwards thrown into temporary confusion, and the Third Division was presently so disorganized as to be unable to resist a counter-charge made against it by the enemy."

The whole line in front of the enemy's infantry in the ravine in front of the Third Division halted after through the narrow belt of timber behind which we had formed, as the trees, brush and terrible shelling had broken the lines and the advanced men where I was laid down to avoid the storm of shells which filled the air till the men got together, which they soon largely did. It was here found the Second Brigade on my right had excusably gone to pieces, the ground in its front being untenable, which caused some delay; but soon we advanced alone without that Brigade, as did the Nineteenth Corps. This was why the Tenth Vermont or guiding regiment, at this time where I was, didn't move forward sooner. The bend to the left in the road is largely a myth. The line of battle wasn't formed at right angles with it which, as the line advanced led to some confusion, as our colors had to be kept on the pike. There was no counter charge in front of where I was in the Tenth Vermont or disorganization, except in the Second Brigade, but what was soon remedied. The enemy could do more effective work by remaining in cover with little loss, which it did.

"At length the commander of the Brigade at our right crossed to our side of the road and urged us to set his men the example. Col. Warner took the responsibility, brought the Brigade to its feet, corrected the alignment, and gave the command to advance, which was promptly obeyed. The Third Divisionfollowed and the line was again in motion. But our point of direction was lost, for we were in advance of our guides, and when it was seen that owing to a curve in the ravine before us the cover on its further side could be reached much sooner by obliquing sharply to the left, we took that direction almost by common consent, and left the road-side."

Why shouldn't Col. Warner with virtually no enemy in his immediate front be able to set an example of advancing his line when the Third Division was up against the real thing, it being confronted with overwhelming numbers of the enemy's infantry in the ravine and artillery back of it in our immediate front pretty much all that confronted the army in that midday assault? The situation in front of our lines is fully explained in this work elsewhere, and an alleged "bend" in the road or a "curve" in the ravine will not suffice to excuse the troops on our immediate left for not at once helping to flank the enemy's infantry from in front of us in the ravine, at once when on high ground across the ravine instead of running off on the field on a comparatively useless easy task and then have to come back. Where was there any infantry of any amount except in the ravine in front of the Third Division? Why not give the Third Division its due? The killed and wounded tell the story. Didn't our Division have about as many killed and wounded as both the First and Second Divisions together, although smaller than either? No fair-minded soldier or person can study the illustrations even, in this work, and fail to see the facts.

"Our whole Brigade, every man at the top of his speed, making for the coveted protection of the hill beyond us, plunged pell mell into the hollow. The troops at our right and left were lost sight of. The ravine was of some considerable width and its bottom was marshy, being the head waters of a little branch of Abraham Creek. The steep slope on its further side was covered with evergreens six or eight feet high. To our intense consternation, as we reached its swampy bottom, we saw at our right, at short pistol range, at least a full regiment of the enemy drawn up in line near the point where the road crosses the hollow, in anticipation of our taking precisely the course we did, and firing coolly, as rapidly as they could load, directly along our line, thus enfilading us completely. Its position is indicated on the plan. The slaughter was for a few moments murderous. We could not retreat, for we should again enter the fire that had been mowing us down in the charge, now cut off by the hill before us. We therefore floundered on, our coherence entirely lost, entered the clusters of evergreens through which the cruel bullets whistled fearfully, and at last, a confused mass at best, those of us who escaped unhurt reached comparative safety under the very crest of the hill, and high above the deadly hollow."

The probabilities are that old soldier-like seeing or suspecting the true situation, the men intuitively or purposely obliqued away to an easier place of attack; at any rate they did it. Yes, the rebel regiment which was seen in the ravine was in front of the left of our brigade, but crossed to the north side of the pike to my front early in the fight leaving no rebel force in the ravine south of the pike in front of the Second Division on the left of ours.

"We now opened fire for the first time during the day, in the direction of the regiment or brigade that had so frightfully thinned our ranks, but they were almost out of reach from us, as well as we from them. At this moment, however, the Third Division approached them and they filed away."

It is difficult to conceive why if the enemy could fire at the union forces here they could not return the compliment, at any rate to one who has so recently studied the ground. It was a good thing the Third Division was 'round to drive the rebs away, otherwise they might have more "frightfully thinned" Col. Walker's ranks. It would be interesting to know exactly how many men Col. Walker lost here.

"When this was discovered, and after gaining breath, our own advance was resumed, but with little pretense at order. Emerging upon the plain before us at the summit of the hill we had climbed, we again turned obliquely towards the road and charged upon a long breastwork filled with rebels, in our immediate front. The retreat of their comrades from the ravine apparently demoralized them; many fled, many more were captured; in fact as we clambered over the parapet it seemed as if the prisoners who then surrendered exceeded in number our entire Brigade."

I saw this movement when the men advanced seemingly to me in an undeployed skirmish line over the open flat ground beyond the ravine not shown in No. 7 illustration, but further to the right. It was a weak force and could not have met any determined resistance from any considerable body; indeed there was but a small force of the enemy's infantry on that part of the field.

"But we did not stop to count them or to care for them. The principal position of the enemy in this portion of the field had now been gained, and we rushed onward toward the distant spires of Winchester, with shouts and cheers, now thoroughly excited by our unexpected success. A battery of the enemy was before us, but it limbered up and retired as we advanced. Several times it turned, fired a round of canister, and resumed its flight. At our left the other Brigades of our Division were seen moving on in our support. At our right an unfortunate ridge now rose, parallel with our line of advance, along the top of which ran the road so often referred to, and which hid our friends from view; we could only hope that they were equally successful, and push wildly forward. A point was reached probably three-fourths of a mile beyond the entrenchments where we had captured the prisoners, when luckily a ditch running across our path suggested cover and a pause. This ditch was reached only by the colors of the Fifth, with perhaps two hundred men from the various regiments. Exhausted with running, they opened fire as vigorously as they could, but a line of rebels was seen gradually collecting in their front, as the fugitives were rallied, and the position held by our troops was presently dangerously threatened. And now to their dismay, the Brigade on the higher ground to their left saw reason for retiring and called for them to follow. What it could mean they did not know, but it seemed prudent to withdraw, if only for the purpose of keeping up the connection. An officer sent to investigate soon reported that at least a Division of the enemy were far behind their right in an orchard, which they supposed had been carried by the Third Division. Orders were given therefore to fall back to the line of the army, following the low ground on the left, thus keeping under cover of the hill at the right, the enemy meantime being absorbed in their movement against Ricketts; and thus the detachment successfully escaped from its dangerous position and re-formed with the balance of the Brigade near the works we had carried, being as before on the right of the other Brigades of our Division, connecting with and at first even in front of the support which was put in to meet the emergency."

Having watched this whole proceeding, which Sheridan saw, too, through his field glass just behind me, after I was wounded and the enemy from the ravine in my front and its artillery were in full retreat, it reads absurdly. The action of the enemy in Col. Walker's front largely depended on that of the enemy in ours, which had been routed and was in full pell mell retreat when Col. Walker's men were advancing in small irregular groups away from the before-mentioned ravine (see No. 7 illustration) they were so seemingly anxious to leave. As a matter of fact if they had swung to the right in and on the high ground west of the ravine, together with the left of our brigade, they would have done much more effective service. The retreating battery mentioned—and others further north not mentioned—retreated because its infantry in the ravine in my front was routed. As a matter of fact these Second Division men were operating comparatively uselessly far on the enemy's rear right flank and were in a dangerous situation as soon as the bulk of the enemy's infantry in my front should reach that neighborhood. I saw this, as did Sheridan, and it was one thing that caused him to put spurs to his horse and dash away to send a staff officer to recall these forces. The five succeeding quoted paragraphs are disingenuously conceived and misleading. They are worse than worthless for historical purposes because mischievous. The Vermont Brigade was too grand a body of men to be mortified by exaggerations and overdrawn situations. The truth is glorious enough, and to write on such a basis is dignified and fair.

"We afterwards learned that a break had taken place on the right which for a time seemed likely to result in complete disaster. The report in our Corps was, that the Nineteenth, advancing through a long stretch of forest and at first successful, had afterwards been repulsed, and fled in disorder, many of the fugitives even going back to the Creek, and that our Third Division had been checked soon after we lost sight of it, presently becoming more or less involved in the flight of the Nineteenth Corps. On the other hand Gen. Emory, commanding the Nineteenth Corps, in a letter published in the *World*, which was fortified with affidavits, insisted that the break began at the right of our Third Division, which led to the turning of his left and the consequent retiring of his Corps. The official reports disagree as much as the letters of the correspondents, who of course reflected the opinions of the several headquarters to which they were attached, and who created considerable ill-feeling by the discrepancies in their accounts, and by their insinuations; the truth is probably between the claims of both, and the real cause of the enemy's temporary success seems to have been the unfortunate bend in the road above mentioned, which interfered with and destroyed the symmetry of our first advance. Our Third Division obliqued to the left as it moved against the enemy, following the order to guide on the road, (there were few or no fences in that vicinity) and so left an interval between its right and the Nineteenth Corps, which appears to have gone in impetuously and with little order; the enemy presently made a counter-charge, and, luckily for them, struck the gap with a heavy force, crumbling off the troops on either side of it, and causing the troops on each side of the interval to think that the others had let the enemy through. The front line of the Nineteenth Corps was almost entirely disorganized, and was replaced by the second line, while only the right of our Third Division was broken up, its left with our own Division merely retiring a short distance under orders, as was necessary in order to keep a continuous front."

This is widely erroneous; Emery's left was somewhat broken at first by the terrific shelling from our front, but it was only in the edge of the shell storm at first when going through the wood. His alleged collapse virtually of the right of our Third Division, or Second Brigade, going through the narrow belt of timber behind which we formed, is correct as before stated, for it was immediately on my right, and I know it; it was largely what we halted and laid down for after getting through the timber. We feared being flanked; but the delay was short, for I almost immediately moved forward with my men and others alone over that flat, unsheltered ground, then being unmercifully swept by artillery and musketry till it was virtually untenable. The Nineteenth Corps instead of obliquing to the left towards us to shorten the interval and help us, intuitively obliqued the other way; but fortunately there was no road or bend in it to blame it to. In my opinion it was as clear a case of shirk as to the left of the Third Division, or a desire to find an easier point to attack. Emery's corps didn't retire that I know of, and our brigade I *know* didn't. The marching of his troops in two long lines was one of the spectacular sights of the day; it was a beautiful feature. It assaulted to the north of the slight divide running east and west, where I saw no infantry nor artillery except a little of the latter far across the breaks. The enfilading infantry and artillery fire from our front at first was about all Emery had to fear, but his Corps soon obliqued away from it. There was *no* counter charge by the enemy in my front or to either side, and in this I am *emphatic*, as well as in the fact that general officers were not where they could see as well as I. There has been more fiction written about this fight than any I was ever in.

"At the critical moment General Wright, who was for the day in command of the Sixth and Nineteenth Corps, though (as he says) 'it was too early in the battle to choose to put in the reserves, still, seeing that the fate of the day depended on the employment of this force,' promptly ordered in the First Division with two batteries; it marched gallantly down, with its full Division front, to the very face of the enemy, relieving the Third Division, which, reforming, presently took up its position still further to the right, where the interval had before been left. Sheridan held back General Upton's Brigade of the First Division until it could strike the flank of the charging column of the rebels, when it made the most remarkable and successful charge of the day, completely breaking up the rebel assault, and permitting our shattered line again to knit itself into coherence. General Upton was there wounded and the brave unostentatious Russell, the idol of the Division he commanded, was shot dead, while personally employed restoring the broken line.

"The two hours following were spent in re-arranging the troops, issuing ammunition, and making dispositions for another advance." * * *

General Russell's Division started to march on the field *en masse* and deployed en route; it was one of the grandest sights of the day or entire war. I never saw such splendid discipline under fire in a large body of men. It didn't relieve our brigade in the sense taken above, but did in partially drawing the enemy's musketry and artillery fire from us, which was appalling and effective. Our Brigade didn't reform. I was close on the enemy's rail breastworks in the ravine with my men leading the assault. There was no chance to reform: it was give and take. Russell's men didn't even get the opportunity of getting near enough the rebels to get satisfaction, for they ran when my men and I were within a rod of their works directly in front. There was no considerable bend in the road or anything else that obliged *my* men either way to any great extent. The enemy ran before Russell was within effective striking or flanking distance. The enemy *didn't* charge. If General Upton assaulted its flank it*wasn't* here. I am *emphatic* in this, for not twenty seconds after I was twice almost simultaneously wounded during the enemy's last volley, it was running for dear life and Sheridan thirty seconds later was on his horse on the high ground close in my rear looking through his field glass to see where the enemy was going to make a second stand, and at other things evidently displeasing to him on his left, where Colonel Walker and the Second Division were. The whole field of active fighting could be seen from here. Five of the battlefield views herein were taken from this point. Colonel Walker is such a graceful, fluent writer it is a pity he couldn't know the whole facts about the battles the Vermont troops were in. His works would doubtless then be charmingly interesting and entertaining.

As several eminent persons, mistakenly as I think, in recent years, in a moment of weakness and gush have classed General R. E. Lee as one of the greatest of modern field marshals, and as the battles of Opequan Creek or Winchester, Va., Sept. 19, 1864, and Gettysburg, Pa., July 1-3, 1863, both of which I have carefully studied, furnish an excellent opportunity for a few pertinent questions as to the ability of Generals Grant, Sheridan and Lee to plan and manage successfully great battles, I cannot refrain from taking up the matter at this point, and I defy any honest man of expert judgment to successfully controvert my stand.

It might as well be said of Sheridan or of Grant, as it has already been of Lee by partial and incompetent judges, that either of the former were the equal of Marlborough or Wellington, and far more truthfully so than of Lee. Had the fortunes of war placed Sheridan in command of the Army of the Potomac at any period of the Civil War, there is no doubt but what that war would have developed in him a field marshal exceeding in dash, ability and brilliancy any military genius of either ancient or modern times. He was a born soldier, unspoilt by training, success or anything else, and was blessed with splendid common sense. *He* was a *genius*, for, says a popular poet:

"There is no balking Genius. Only death
Can silence it or hinder. While there's breath
Or sense of feeling, it will spurn the sod,
And lift itself to glory, and to God.
The acorn sprouted—weeds nor flowers can choke
The certain growth of th' upreaching oak."

One secret of Sheridan's success lay largely in his ability to so plan a battle as to fight his whole command *effectively* all at once, and in such a way that with his dash and unexpected *coup de main*, the enemy was usually whipped before the fight was fairly commenced. With Sheridan in command during the Civil War, President Lincoln would never have had to urge action on the part of the Army of the Potomac as with McClellan and others, except Grant, when ready to fight, nor would it have been fought in detail, which was invariably a fatal fault with both armies, for Sheridan didn't fight that way; there were no unfought reserves in his army. When he struck it was with so much method, dash, determination and judgment it brought brilliant results, such as astonished even his own army, which always expected victory, as well as the enemy and every one else; and in consequence he could accomplish more with fewer men than any other General in the army; not only because he used his force to the best advantage by fighting it all at once, but because his personal magnetism, or hypnotism, enthused the men and gave them confidence, which is a great thing in battle; besides, they had implicit faith in his ability, splendid judgment and quick perception on the battlefield, which are indispensable gifts in a great General; and when combined with an alert, active temperament such as his, it was *grand*. *He* was a *great* field marshal. This is proven from the fact that anything he undertook in the Civil War was not only *well* done if decently supported, but he proved himself grandly equal to any occasion on the field of battle, wherever the fortunes of war placed him—not tamely so, but *brilliantly*; he electrified his men as well as the world by his splendid dash, pluck and surprisingly overwhelming victories. A slight reverse not only left him undaunted but, like a raging lion, it seemed to arouse his wonderful gifts and raise him to such sublime heights it awed one; so that the moment the eye of his command caught a vision of him at any distance on the battlefield, his very pose and action was such it electrified and imbued his men with the same spirit of conquer or die that dominated him, and no enemy could or ever did stand for any length of time before his intrepid command.

Who but Sheridan, as at Cedar Creek, Va., Oct. 19, 1864, just a month to a day after his splendid victory at Opequan Creek, Sept. 19, 1864, or Winchester, Va., as now more properly known, could have rallied a defeated and routed army en route to the front and after and so enthused it in the act, simply by dashing, alert and crafty through its broken ranks after a twenty mile race with time from Winchester, with flashing eyes, bared head and waving hat, on a spirited foaming horse, shouting to his men: "Get back into line, men! Get into line, *quick*! We can lick 'em! We can lick h——l out of 'em yet!" and do it almost at once, even as brilliantly so as at Winchester a month previous? How often are such things done? Such a man outclasses all others in military history, not excepting Wellington or Marlborough, for such a man as Sheridan is without a peer as a field marshal in the annals of warfare; and had he been found sooner and given greater responsibilities he would not only have surely proved it, but would have more fully electrified the world than he did and have been its idol as a military genius and hero for all time.

He or Grant would never have used such woefully poor judgment as to have assaulted an army equally as valiant, splendidly posted, fully as large, if not larger than their own, across an open, level space without cover quite a mile in extent, as Lee did at Gettysburg on July 3, 1864. If that act showed ability, good judgment, or a military genius, then I am lacking in mature sound judgment, and my lifetime of military training, including my three years and threescore battles or more in the Civil War and in Indian wars, has been in vain. This would be equally true even though the armies had been equal in numbers. General Longstreet's suggestion to Lee to place his army on General Meade's flank between him and Washington would have been a splendid substitute for Pickett's forlorn charge. It was abler and just what Grant did with Lee hardly a year later, successfully and repeatedly and forced Lee back to Richmond and Petersburg, as the world now knows, which indicates superior generalship both on Grant's part as well as Longstreet's.

Would either Grant or Sheridan have lost their cavalry for several days, as Lee did, when on such a campaign in an enemy's country or anywhere else? Would either, with three such splendid cavalry divisions as Meade, not have used a part of one division if necessary to have patrolled barely seventy-five miles between York, Pa., or the Susquehanna, and the Potomac river, in order to detect any movement by the enemy on Washington? Would this have made the Union Commander, whoever he might have been, timid about moving to any point where battle was offered, fearing a fake attack by Lee in order to cover a movement on Washington or Baltimore? One brigade would have established a line of patrol posts less than a quarter of a mile apart of six men each, which would have detected at once any movement south by Lee, or if preferred, posts one-eighth of a mile apart of three men each.

Would Grant or Sheridan have remained so near a great battle as at Gettysburg, July 1, 1864, and not have furnished an opportunity for another soul-stirring poem like "Sheridan's Ride"? When they were informed that the enemy had attacked their forces barely three hours' ride away, would they have loitered a whole day away like dullards, as both army commanders did at Gettysburg? Aye! either would have made the ride in two hours or even less, and even though their steeds were as black as night, on their arrival at Gettysburg they would have been as white as snow or as foam could have made them; and, still better, they would not only have known, too, through their cavalry, spies, etc., for we were at home among friends, where Lee's army corps were, but when each broke camp to concentrate at Gettysburg, and their own corps close by them would have been there in season to have met the enemy in at least equal numbers, instead of being outnumbered all day July 1, two to one, as was the case. If necessary, too, as at Opequan Creek, Sept. 19, 1864, the different corps would have marched at 2 o'clock instead of 8 o'clock A. M. or even earlier if thought necessary.

Was there any excuse for the Confederates not driving the Union forces from the field in a rout on July first? They would have done so, too, except that their forces were fought in detail, its reserves not even being brought into action when needed. Did Ewell take the best advantage of his opportunities? The enemy outnumbered us quite two to one the first day from first to last after the battle commenced, but still at the first dash of two brigades of our Infantry—Wadsworth's Division—against two brigades of the enemy, when Reynolds was killed, we placed *hors de combat* over half of each of their brigades and captured Archer, a brigade commander; and still the enemy had two brigades in immediate reserve as support, but they were not used. This is what I call fighting an army in detail, a total waste of material. In case Sheridan hadn't thrown his support or reserve—Russell's division—into the fight at the right moment at Winchester, Va., Sept. 19, 1864, his results would have been equally as ignominious as his victory was brilliant, because he did use his reserve correctly on that occasion; and so it would have been with the enemy at Gettysburg had it used its reserve. It would probably have captured many of our men and driven the balance of them from the field in a rout, as Sheridan did Early at Winchester, Sept. 19, 1864; there was nothing to prevent it.

Does Lee deserve being classed among the greatest field marshals of modern times for such field marshalship as was displayed at the first day's fighting at Gettysburg? But, says the incompetent critic who forms his conclusions from gush, policy, favoritism, sentiment, or weakly otherwise, instead of for the sake of truth and correct history, Lee wasn't there! Aye! but wasn't it an *alert* Commander's—a *genius's*—business to have been there? What was he in Pennsylvania for or selected and paid for handling such an important matter to the Confederacy for? Who gave the order to concentrate for battle at Gettysburg but he? Does not every experienced soldier know that under such circumstances no one can tell exactly at what moment a battle will commence? And would not an alert, sagacious commander have made a forced night ride in order to have been with the first of his forces on the field? Lee *knew* he was going to fight if the enemy would fight him, but Meade didn't; hence Lee knew exactly what to do. A *great* field marshal would have been more alert—on hand—it seems to me.

Lee commanded in person the second day at Gettysburg, and not only failed to attack early in the morning, when he should, but, as usual, when he did, fought his army in detail using Longstreet's corps largely against two of our corps in turn which, being overwhelmed by numbers, and Meade failing to reinforce them, as he should or not have sent them where he did, they were of course forced back to their proper positions onto the correct line of battle beyond which they should never have been advanced, and with a sagacious, alert, competent commander would not have been except the whole army advanced together in a general assault which it should have done anyway after Wright's brigade was repulsed.

From first to last in the battle of Gettysburg, I fail to see anything to commend on the enemy's part in any of its generals except in Longstreet; nor on the Union side so far as Meade was concerned, but do in many others, and especially Buford, Reynolds, Doubleday and Howard, each of whom in turn successively commanded our forces in the order mentioned without being routed, against great odds under exceedingly trying circumstances owing to Meade's failure apparently, to fully grasp the situation *fourteen miles away*. It shows what splendid fighters Buford, Reynolds, Doubleday and Howard's men were to stand off double their number for an entire day, with what help they got from Schurz's men.

That Lee did not grasp the situation is evident or else he would have assaulted our lines early on the morning of July second before Meade's forces arrived on the field. It is said he did give the order to do so, but if he had been a *great* military genius wouldn't he have *seen* that it was done? Instead of this owing largely probably, to Meade's lack of alertness and enterprise, Lee from lack of sagacity became apparently dizzy and unbalanced, as was most of his command, because of his apparently misunderstood partial successes, of the first and second days' fights, and was so criminally lacking in good judgment on the third day as to be led into the mistake of ordering Pickett's charge which, for obvious reasons, could only result in calamity to the Southern cause. This even an amateur soldier of ordinary judgment should have been able to have foreseen.

My sympathy in a military and every other sense so far as the enemy is concerned, goes out to Longstreet sitting on the fence with bowed head, a picture of despair and blasted hopes probably not only on account of a useless slaughter of his brave men which he foresaw, but because of a loss of faith in the ability of his chief and in consequence the loss eventually of the cause of the Confederacy; and what thoughtful military man of experience can't see what else for scapegoats are always found for such occasions on which to try and lay the blame. But it won't do with ripe scientific military men nor would it with Lee were he living, for when too late he doubtless saw his mistake, as he acknowledged like the *man* he *always* was to his veterans, when returning from the slaughter after the assault that the calamity of defeat was all his fault. How pathetic!

Longstreet's heart was doubtless breaking when Pickett seemingly too thoughtless to comprehend the situation rode up to Longstreet and then "gaily" to his command in the midst of the artillery fire preceding the assault, and asked if he should commence the charge. Longstreet's heart and tongue were doubtless as good as paralyzed or at any rate refused to perform their function, and he answered with a sad and silent nod.

How any military student of age and extended experience in warfare—for few others are expert judges—who ever studied the country north of the Potomac river, field and battle of Gettysburg or Antietam, can class Lee with Marlborough and Wellington, it is difficult to understand; and Lee's mistakes here were by no means his only. He never found his superior, though, on the battlefield until he met Grant when, for the first time, he found a *genius* who didn't know what it was to retreat before the Army of Northern Virginia, nor did Lee ever advance again but to be checkmated. Prior to that the Army of the Potomac had taken care of itself single-handed—so to speak—as it would have done anywhere after 1862, if placed in line and told to fight, if let alone: it would have carried any man at its head through to victory, as it did Meade at Gettysburg, and especially in such a place as that when so much depended upon it.

It was the intrepid men with the guns, many of whom were more competent in battle than some of their officers, who largely won the battles, and not unfrequently because of greater physical endurance and undaunted courage led in the hottest places by scores in all assaults, for otherwise but few battles would have been won. To be in such company was an inspiration for such men knew no fear and they were not reckless either, but coolly alert in taking every advantage of surroundings and conditions, as well as of the enemy. Such needed no officer to lead them, but they would be devoted to one who had the pluck to go with them, and fortunate was he who was strong enough to put fear behind him and do it. It is more elevating morally to be born with such a gift than rich.

Anyone who has read Lincoln's telegrams and letters to Meade imploring him not to let Lee escape across the Potomac after Pickett's suicidal charge which is only exceeded in American War history in lack of ability by Abercrombie's maladministration of his Ticonderoga campaign in the Colonial war in 1758. cannot possibly think Grant or Sheridan would have showed so little military genius; and it is a disappointment to one in mature years who fought continually under Meade in youth about two years to find that he was so lacking in sagacity and military enterprise as to not take advantage of his great opportunities. He was all right when a subordinate, but out of place as chief.

It was largely lack of ability on the part of commanders of the Army of the Potomac as military men until Lee met Grant, which in contrast makes Lee appear to some unread in civil war history so much more brilliant than he really was as a military man. It was very generally supposed during the war it was interference from Washington that caused a lack of success on the part of the Army of the Potomac, but official correspondence between Lincoln and others at Washington with the different commanders of the Army of the Potomac published since the Civil War shows that it was largely due to their downright ignorance of how to conduct a campaign until Grant took command, which rendered it absolutely necessary to interfere. To a man of long expert military training some of the questions asked by commanders of Lincoln and others, are astonishing. They not only show a lack of judgment, self reliance and ability, but in some cases utter incompetency; and when such didn't asked to be relieved from force of circumstances, they *had* to be. In most cases it was disingenuously claimed by the incumbent that they were handicapped by the Washington authorities, which is probably what largely created the false impression that they were much imposed upon. The government doubtless considerately thought it could not afford to let the truth be known for obvious reasons, and besides it was doubtless thought such men might be efficient in a less responsible position in cases of emergency and their usefulness would be impaired if the real facts were made known; hence the position of Lincoln and others near to him in Washington in such a respect was not only a noble self sacrifice, but must have been even more trying than at any time or even now generally known. Under such circumstances any ordinary commander of the Confederate Army would appear to good advantage as Lee did, which, to any but one who is expert, is misleading. He had military talent but it even was never fully developed. His was *not* Genius:

"Genius spreads its wings
And soars beyond itself, or selfish things.
Talent has need of stepping-stones; some cross,
Some cheated purpose, some great pain or loss,

Must lay the groundwork, and arouse ambition,
Before it labors onward to fruition."

But Lee never in war arose to such sublime heights if indeed ever in a military sense.

Even Longstreet's Chief of Artillery, General Alexander, a man of splendid sense and judgment, in his "Military Memoirs of a Confederate," holds that the real crisis of the War did not occur until Grant's movement against Petersburg, which is correct, and that his strategy in that campaign was well planned and successfully executed. He acknowledges that Grant completely outmanoeuvered Lee for the last three days during the Petersburg movement, thus saving his army from attack by the combined forces of Lee and Beauregard, which is also correct. Imagine Lee's disappointment when he found out what had been going on after Grant had crossed the James river! It completely checkmated him, even his last kick—Early's Shenandoah Valley campaign—proving worse than a failure it so weakened Lee's army. Think you Lee then thought himself a greater field marshal than Grant? Or after being continually flanked by him from the Rapidan to Petersburg and later to Appomattox where his surrender occurred?

In bringing up this matter at this opportune time when contrasts can be sharply and tellingly drawn as at Winchester and Gettysburg, my purpose has not been to disparage anyone unfairly, but to get at the truth as I see it for the sake of true history. So long a time has elapsed since the war that I look upon it and its actors dispassionately, and I can award praise or censure on either side whenever deserved with calmness and impartiality. Therefore if, as a veteran, I have advanced any new ideas on a subject necessarily somewhat perplexing to the general public, at any period, my object in treating it will have been accomplished.

Possibly there may be some excuse for such as did not fight in the Army of the Potomac three years and have not read the latest history on the Civil War and made it a study, erring in their estimates of the leaders in that conflict. I always, even during the war, thought the South had abler men to command its army of Northern Virginia even in that army than Lee, but none more lovely in disposition and character. He was a good man and good but *not* a *great* general; and, much less, in the same class with Marlborough, Wellington, and others of modern wars, or Grant, Sheridan, and others of the Civil War, which facts prove. Any man who is a military expert familiar with the subject both from participation, history and study, if of good judgment and honest, will readily concede this. Lee's distinguished lineage has nothing to do with his military history. He should be judged on his own merits in such a way, but his antecedents and charming personal character seemingly makes it difficult for most writers to place him in a military sense where he belongs. In my opinion, all things being equal, he was no match for Grant.

TUESDAY, Sept. 20, 1864.

My wounds were very painful during the night, my lips and face are terribly swollen and my jaws are in shocking condition, but I'm thankful it is no worse. My side and chest are very lame, but I hope it is nothing more serious than a bruise or contusion. Lieut. Hill has had his leg amputated, but I don't think he can live, the stump is so short—poor, brave, gallant, natty Hill with the most of life before him. Sheridan's loss was 5018 of which 4300 were killed and wounded. Early's loss was about the same. About 850 of his wounded fell into our hands. Our division lost 600 in killed and wounded and seventeen are missing, more than both of the other two divisions of our corps together. Our regiment lost twelve killed and forty-six wounded. Sheridan captured two thousand prisoners, five pieces of artillery and nine battle flags. Generals Rhodes and Godwin of Kershaw's Division were killed, and General York lost an arm. I saw Major Dillingham at a distance as he lay stricken, when I entered the hospital grounds yesterday. He was no shirk in battle but valiant. We feel like sparing him least of any, and had not looked for it, therefore it is a great shock. Only a moment before the order to advance he was talking with several officers near me and was in the best of spirits which, it occurred to me at the time, greatly contrasted with my feeling for I never dreaded more to go into battle. I was greatly but silently depressed.

WEDNESDAY, Sept. 21, 1864.

I was moved up to Winchester yesterday with the rest of the wounded. The city is one vast hospital—in fact nearly every house is used to accommodate the wounded, and it was a smart place of about four thousand before the war, but now is one of about ten thousand, owing to this battle. Most of the wounded officers were left at Taylor's Hotel. The surgeons are very busy amputating limbs. It is said that there are over 1300 wounded in this hotel. My wounds are doing well considering but are very painful. Oh, what a horrible sight! I have seen piles of arms and legs today at the hospital thrown from the windows of operating rooms as big as haycocks. It's a shocking sight! So many lying about dead, too! It is rumored that we have again given Early battle and completely routed his forces capturing a large number of prisoners, but this needs confirmation.

THURSDAY, Sept. 22, 1864.

Through the kindness of Chaplain Haynes who has been indefatigable in looking after the wounded, I have today engaged board in a private family, a Quaker lady—Mrs. Wright—the mother of the celebrated Rebekah Wright, who sent Sheridan information of the enemy before the battle Sept. 19, by a colored man in a piece of tinfoil hid in his mouth, that Kershaw's division and twelve pieces of artillery had returned to Lee, and that the enemy wasn't as strong as supposed. She has a schoolroom at home here, is a teacher, and very solicitous for our wounded—a modest, sensible, interesting lady. They are very nice people, and exceedingly kind. My wound is healing rapidly, and the swelling has disappeared fast within the last twenty-four hours, but I can't speak or eat, taking gruel through a tube only, and my jaws are paining me. Lieut. Hill is doing well, and may get well, but the test will come in a day or so. It's rumored that we've again whipped the enemy but I doubt it; weather fine. My wounds are very stiff this evening.

Friday, Sept. 23, 1864.

Well, I must confess that a good soft pillow is more comfortable for one to rest a sore head on than an oak log; rested very well last night considering the condition of my mouth. Mrs. Wright is very kind. I wish Lieut. Hill could be moved up here. A long army train loaded with wounded started for Harper's Ferry early this morning, also about 1500 prisoners. Captain Goodrich and Lieut. H. W. Kingsley of the Brigade staff called to see me to-day. My wound is improving. I went with Rebeckah Wright and another young Union lady—very pretty—to see Lieut. D. G. Hill this forenoon. He is very gallant to ladies, always, and seemed cheerful, but I think the poor fellow assumes it. He is a patient sufferer. I have to be for I can't utter a word; am termed the interesting patient by the ladies, and get lots of sympathy.

Saturday, Sept. 24, 1864.

I am expecting to go to Harper's Ferry; reported to the Surgeon in charge this morning as directed, but the train hasn't come from the front yet, therefore I shan't probably get off today. My wound has been very painful this afternoon —in fact more painful than it's ever been yet. The Eighty-seventh Pennsylvania went through the city this afternoon en route for home. Well, let them go, they are deserving of such joy! It's a good regiment. My wound has gotten very sore and painful and don't give me a moment's peace. My system is beginning to feel the strain, too, and my tongue seems paralyzed yet. I can't utter a word. At any rate I'm not noisy company for anyone—not even the ladies here who are very sympathetic.

Sunday, Sept. 25, 1864.

I did not sleep much last night my wounds were so *very* painful. I removed some of the old fractures or splinters of the teeth and jaws that were left, about 3 o'clock a. m. with my fingers, and after that my face was easier and I rested some. I started in a private wagon from Winchester at 11 o'clock a. m. for

Harper's Ferry, and at dark was still on the road near Charlestown *very* tired; had no scares from guerrillas; am beginning to feel weak, having eaten nothing solid since I was wounded, but I was pretty vigorous. The shock to my system has been greater than I was aware of, now that the excitement is over.

MONDAY, Sept. 26, 1864.

Tonight finds me in the hotel at Harper's Ferry waiting for my leave of absence which I expect tomorrow; arrived last night at 10 o'clock tired and lame, but not discouraged although my mouth was sore and painful. The swelling has largely gone, and I can eat a little quite comfortably if the food is soft, but I couldn't if I wasn't nearly famished. Major Goddard—our paymaster—paid me today. I expected to have to go to Washington.

TUESDAY, Sept. 27, 1864.

O, what a delightful morning! And the scenery here about Harper's Ferry is so grand that it makes it all the more enjoyable. Of course, I awoke in fine spirits for how could I help it? I thought I was to start for home at 1 o'clock p. m. but on going to the hospital, I found that my leave had not been sent over for approval therefore I can't go until tomorrow. The wagon train has started for the front again. I am sure I shall start for Vermont tomorrow. Sometimes I almost think it would be a good thing if some of the Adjutants General could be wounded, too, perhaps they would see to it then that wounded men's applications for leave to go home were not delayed.

WEDNESDAY, Sept. 28, 1864.

It has been an anxious morning for me; went over to Sandy Hook and waited until 11 o'clock a. m. when the clerk handed me my leave, and I must say, I felt like a new man. I hurried back to Harper's Ferry and found Mr. Hicks there in search of his brother Lieut. John Hicks of my regiment, who was wounded in the thigh at Fisher's Hill. I waited until 4 o'clock p. m. and took the cars for Baltimore, but the train was delayed and it did not arrive there till 2 o'clock a. m. Sept. 29.

THURSDAY, Sept. 29, 1864.

Stopped at the Eutaw House last night; arose at 6 o'clock a. m. from necessity and went shopping; got breakfast at 8.30 o'clock a. m. and took the cars for New York City; arrived at the Astor House, New York, about 8 o'clock p. m.; looks like rain; city much excited; good news from Grant.

FRIDAY, Sept. 30, 1864.

I intended to have taken the 7 o'clock a. m. train, but overslept; left on the 10.30 o'clock a. m. train up the Hudson river. The scenery is the most beautiful

I have ever seen; arrived at Albany about sundown; changed cars at Troy for Rutland; arrived there at 9 o'clock p. m. Ed. Russell has been with me today.

SATURDAY, Oct. 1, 1864.

Stayed in Rutland last night; took the 4 o'clock a. m. train for Burlington, but to my disgust found it to be a freight; arrived at Burlington at noon; took the 1 o'clock p. m. train for Montpelier; arrived there at 4 o'clock p. m.; stopped at Burnham's Hotel; found Carl Wilson; hasn't changed much in three years nor Montpelier; think a boil is coming on my ankle; am half sick.

SUNDAY, Oct. 2, 1864.

Am in good old Vermont at last, if I have got a boil coming. Major Dillingham's remains arrived in Waterbury last night, and the funeral services have been today, but it has rained hard all day. I am not able to be out. Carl Wilson and Frank French called to see me today. My boil is very painful; have not been out of the house; would like to have gone to Major Dillingham's funeral but can't get about till my boil breaks on my ankle. I'm ill, too.

MONDAY, Oct. 3, 1864.

Cloudy and foggy; have taken cold in my face; ankle worse today, too; have not been outdoors. Orry Blanchard has been in to see me; saw Mr. Walters in the barroom, also Mr. Hanson, but did not know the former. Sergeant Hogle has called. My wound is paining me more than usual tonight; jaws in bad condition; hope the fractures will heal all right. I thought the Johnnies had shot my whole chin off at first; it was paralyzed a long time, and don't feel right yet; it must be the jaw.

TUESDAY, Oct. 4, 1864.

Cloudy and gloomy; have been up to Carl's drug store, but found it rather difficult walking; am not feeling very well; went up to Carl's again this afternoon for pills; remained on the bed all afternoon; didn't go down to tea; Carl Wilson called this afternoon; wound pains me *very* badly tonight.

WEDNESDAY, Oct. 5, 1864.

Somewhat better. Mrs. George Watson called to see me yesterday evening, but I was unable to receive lady callers, although I did not know it was her; went up to the office this afternoon; found Jo Watson and took a stroll up to the State House; getting it ready for the Legislature; am going to Williamstown in the morning.

THURSDAY, Oct. 6, 1864.

Am feeling very much better this morning; very foggy till about 9 o'clock a.

m. when the sun came out brightly; got a team about 10 o'clock a. m. and Jo Watson took me to James Burnham's place in Williamstown; arrived at Barre about noon; called at Mrs. David Mower's; no one there but Hattie Glover; did not get out; arrived at James' at 3 o'clock p. m.; all well; took them by surprise.

FRIDAY, Oct. 7, 1864.

Well, it seems good to get out in the country among relatives, where it's quiet; my wound is worse than I thought it would be. My teeth and jaws are feeling very badly and my lip looks irritated. Ezra and Ro Benedict have been up to see me today. Ro has got some beautiful little children. James has gone to Bradford to the fair.

SATURDAY, Oct. 8, 1864.

Rained all forenoon; gloomy day, but have passed the time pleasantly; am reading Aurora Floyd, but like East Lynne, better; pleasant but showery. James commenced reading East Lynne this evening; mouth gaining rapidly.

SUNDAY, Oct. 9, 1864.

Gloomy morning; am feeling better. Ryland Seaver has been down to see me this morning. Andrew Burnham and wife also called this afternoon; think they are looking a little worn; marriage without means is evidently not a bed of roses even for vigorous people on a country hillside farm. Rodney Seaver has also been in to see me, too; has married since I've been in the army. He is another good man, but Ryle and I have always been firm friends and always shall be. The three Seaver brothers are straight, reliable, splendid men.

MONDAY, Oct. 10, 1864.

A cold night for the season; froze quite hard; snow on the ground this morning; don't seem much like Virginia climate; weather much moderated tonight; looks like southern storm. Alma Seaver has been in to see me this afternoon. My mouth wound is nearly healed externally, but it is very stiff, awkward and clumsy; don't feel right—the jaws ache; cooler tonight.

TUESDAY, Oct. 11, 1864.

Northwest wind; fair, comfortable day. James has gone to John Pane's auction; have been down to Washington village this evening with Jim; called to see his eldest sister—Mrs. Pepper; finished reading Aurora Floyd this afternoon; expect Pert this evening; beautiful night; not much thrilling diary data out here on this peaceful hillside Vermont farm.

WEDNESDAY, Oct. 12, 1864.

Rather a gloomy morning; stormed till about 9 o'clock a. m. then cleared off, but snowed this afternoon; wrote Dr. Clark. Pert didn't come; very dull.

THURSDAY, Oct. 13, 1864.

Snowed all day; seems quiet after such an exciting life in the army. Mr. Lyman Drury brought Pert down this evening. Byron Bradley writes that Uncle Pierce and Cousin Abby are somewhere in the East. My face wound troubles me tonight and I guess always will by spells.

FRIDAY, Oct. 14, 1864.

Well, I wonder if winter's come! It has rained and snowed all day; face badly swollen today, but my jaws don't ache much for which I'm thankful; shall go down to Aunt Polly Howe's to-morrow if it don't storm. It's snowing tonight.

SATURDAY, Oct. 15, 1864.

It snowed nearly all the forenoon. In the afternoon it was quite comfortable; thawed considerable, but night still finds the ground covered with snow. My teeth and jaws have troubled me constantly, but I feel more comfortable this evening; shall go down to Aunt Howe's in the morning. Oh, dear! I shall be glad when I get so that I can feel like other folks. It is still thawing this evening.

SUNDAY, Oct. 16, 1864.

Ryland came down to see me early this morning. Fernando Thompson brought me some letters; got one from Dr. J. H. Jones; friends in Chelsea all well; am at Uncle Howe's to-night; Jim brought us down this forenoon; no one home but Uncle Howe; no change in Williamstown; terribly quiet.

MONDAY, Oct. 17, 1864.

Went over to see Cousin George Simons last evening, who is in poor health, as well as Cousin Martha. Aunt Sarah is usually well; weather fair. Aunt Polly Howe seems depressed; expect she's anxious about me; arrived at Mr. David Mower's this evening; came down in Mr. Snow's crowded stage very uncomfortably.

TUESDAY, Oct. 18, 1864.

Cloudy with wind; have been to Montpelier with Mrs. David Mower and Cousin Pert; had a good time; dined with the Watsons; visited several Tenth Vermont men in the afternoon at the hospital; got my dress coat and overcoat at Woolson's; got home about dark; rather cold tonight.

WEDNESDAY, Oct. 19, 1864.

Cloudy, dismal day; took Cousin Pert and Hattie Glover out to Cousin David

Smith's in the afternoon, and visited at Ann Martin's in the evening; returned to David's for the night; very dark with blinding rain and snow, but got home safe; have enjoyed the day.

THURSDAY, Oct. 20, 1864.

Weather cloudy and gloomy; started about 9 o'clock a. m. to take Hattie Glover home, then took Pert to call on Phineas Thompson's family, and then in the afternoon we went to John Wilson's. It's always a pleasure to see Mr. and Mrs. Wilson though a sad duty since Em and the other children died. Pert and I called on Helen Thompson, and I in the evening on Mrs. Oromal Dodge. Coming home our wheel set over which we had quite a frolic, but we arrived safely.

FRIDAY, Oct. 21, 1864.

It has seemed a long day; have been in the village all day; called on Charley French; wound fairly easy today. Pert, Hattie Glover and I went up to the Academy Lyceum this evening; students much younger than before the war; probably older boys in the army; dark and gloomy to-night.

SATURDAY, Oct. 22, 1864.

Quite a fine day. James Burnham came down after Pert this morning. Cousin Hattie Burnham is ill with diphtheria. I called on Mr. and Mrs. Bliss this forenoon; am to stay at Nate Harrington's tonight. Carl Wilson came up from Montpelier about 8 o'clock p. m. Several of the girls came in in the evening and we had a pleasant time.

SUNDAY, Oct. 23, 1864.

Went with Carl up to his father's this morning; intended to go to church this afternoon, but didn't get dinner in season; had a good visit with Mr. and Mrs. John Wilson. Herbert and Laura Leonard, old schoolmates, called; have grown greatly; was glad to see them. Carl and I stopped at David Mower's in the afternoon.

MONDAY, Oct. 24, 1864.

Pert, Hattie Glover and I started for Montpelier en route for Burlington this morning at 6 o'clock in a crowded stage. They were on a frolic; had a half dozen bandboxes in the front hall they pretended had got to go, because they knew I objected to traveling with such. We had some backwoods passengers which amused the girls greatly; arrived in Montpelier at 9 o'clock a. m.; shopped some and took the 11 o'clock a. m. train for Burlington. Fred Johonnott met us at the depot, who is engaged to Hattie, and took us to the Stanton House; saw Hidden Hand played at the theatre in the evening.

Tuesday, Oct. 25, 1864.

Went to see Dr. Thayer about getting my leave extended about 10 o'clock a. m.; found him at his house but cranky; would not, to my surprise, give me a certificate for extension of leave. My wound is not yet fully healed, the stitches are still in, it's sensitive, inflamed and sore, can't eat solid food, am not fit to go to the front, and I'm no malingerer either. It would teach Dr. Thayer something to get in a hot fight and be wounded. I never did like bandbox doctors, anyway! I'm afraid the board of surgeons at Annapolis, Md. will discharge me for *they* are practical men. I'm disgusted with Thayer! All I need is a reasonable time for my wound to mend. A man with a part of his head shot away can't be expected to be fit for duty a month after. If I shirked battle, I suppose Thayer would extend my sick leave! That's the way such things usually go! Merit don't count though, with testy doctors if approached too soon after breakfast. If I were a toady in manner or reality, I suppose I could get anything, but I'm only a plain, presentable, unassuming country lad while Thayer impresses me as an aristocrat. Ed. Russell has taken me to ride about Burlington, a very pretty little city; took the noon train for Montpelier; shall go up and call professionally on Dr. James in the morning; he'll give me a certificate.

Wednesday, Oct. 26, 1864.

This has been the first pleasant day I've seen in Vermont since I came home; met Captain P. D. Blodget on the street; was glad to see him for he is a nice, *fair* man. His wounded arm is looking very badly; do not think he will ever return to the regiment again. I went up to the hospital with him and he gave me an introduction to Dr. James who examined my wounds and gave me a certificate for thirty days extension of sick leave; have been up to the State House this evening to hear Mrs. Chester read.

Thursday, Oct. 27, 1864.

It's not quite as pleasant this morning as yesterday; had Dr. Forbush operate on my game jaws, teeth, etc., this forenoon; took ether and I must say that I have no desire to ever take any more. The doctor tells me my upper jaw is very badly injured. I suspected it but hoped it might be the crushed teeth which gave me so much pain; have been sick all the forenoon from the effects of the ether. When I came out from under its influence I was crying like a great booby, for just at that time I was living over my illness of typhoid fever when I was reported dead at Rockville, Md. in the winter of 1862-63, and I thought I was all alone among strangers. It was more real, though, as I was delirious at Rockville, and don't recall any such genuine anguish as I was experiencing when I awoke from the effects of ether. To awake from such hallucinations to the realities of life comparatively well was a remarkable experience; it dazed me for a moment on coming back to the world, but I rallied soon on looking at the doctor and Pert and saw them relievedly smiling at my surprised look and manner. I went to a band concert tonight, and stayed with Carl Wilson.

F<small>RIDAY</small>, Oct. 28, 1864.

I did not get up till 10 o'clock a. m.; am feeling some better this morning; rained hard all day. Roger Bixby brought me up to Barre this afternoon. The Smith band came up to give a concert but as it rained so hard it postponed it till next week.

S<small>ATURDAY</small>, Oct. 29, 1864.

Fair day. The Smith band came up and gave a serenade this forenoon; have had a pleasant time at Mr. West's. News came today that Captain L. D. Thompson of Waterbury was decapitated by a solid shot in battle at Cedar Creek, Va., and that Adjutant Wyllys Lyman, Captain C. F. Nye, Lieuts. G. E. Davis, G. P. Welch, A. W. Fuller and B. B. Clark were also wounded there. We have had seven officers killed, twelve wounded and two captured since the first of June, making twenty-one in all, the regiment's full quota not including non-combatants, were they all present which is never the case, being thirty-four. Who will say we haven't stood up to the rack? I guess they intend to kill us all off—men and all! I may not have included all the casualties among the officers in the foregoing. Poor Dillingham, Stetson and Thompson! They were my original officers in Company B—all gone—killed in battle. They were good fellows—intrepid and valiant to a fault. Lieut. Stetson was a considerate, kindly friend, and a man who was fair and manly, and never took a mean, unfair advantage of anyone so far as I know; he won my esteem. I became fond of Captain Thompson; he grew on me constantly until we were good friends, and the manner of his unfortunate death shocks me. Poor fellow! I sincerely regret his tragic end; he was brave, always genial, obliging and friendly. They grew to like, respect and esteem me, and I have lost three staunch friends—probably among the best in the regiment with the officers. They have all been martyrs to the cause of the Union. May their souls go marching on and finally welcome mine in eternity!

S<small>UNDAY</small>, Oct. 30, 1864.

A beautiful day; have been to church twice. Mr. Bliss preached two excellent sermons. He always preaches well; is a remarkably gifted, brainy, interesting speaker from the pulpit. Dr. Carpenter's funeral was this afternoon from the Congregational Church. Mr. Beckley's funeral services were attended this afternoon from the M. E. Church; beautiful evening; have been up to the cemetery with Mr. and Mrs. Mower.

M<small>ONDAY</small>, Oct. 31, 1864.

Stormed this forenoon; went up to see Nate and Ardelia Harrington and remained all night; called on Mrs. Patterson and Mr. Hiram Blanchard's family. Captain L. D. Thompson's remains arrived at Waterbury this evening; funeral tomorrow; cold tonight; army news good this evening.

TUESDAY, Nov. 1, 1864.

Mrs. Charles Scott, Ardelia Harrington and Cousin Pert have gone to Montpelier. I came by stage to Chelsea and am with Dr. J. H. Jones tonight; left So. Barre at 11.30 o'clock a. m.; rode to Tunbridge with the doctor to visit a young lady ill with typhoid fever this evening.

WEDNESDAY, Nov. 2, 1864.

Cool and pleasant this morning. Dr. Jones has gone to Tunbridge; have spent the day with Dr. Bagley's family; shall remain here over night; called on Mrs. Hayward and her daughter, Susan, this evening.

THURSDAY, Nov. 3, 1864.

It's a lovely morning; went to Tunbridge with Dr. Jones; fine evening; am to stay at Mr. Isaac Merrill's tonight.

FRIDAY, Nov. 4, 1864.

Has rained hard all day. Ike's a little off on the war; went to the village about 4 o'clock p. m.; called on Mrs. Lyman Hinkley, am at Mrs. Hayward's tonight.

SATURDAY, Nov. 5, 1864.

Have been to see Jo Watson to-day; weather cold and blustering all day; am with Dr. J. H. Jones tonight; he's visiting a patient; am alone.

SUNDAY, Nov. 6, 1864.

Left Chelsea at 10 o'clock a. m. for Barre; Jo Watson brought me over; attended church this afternoon, heard an excellent sermon by Rev. F. S. Bliss; called on Mrs. Oromal Dodge this evening.

MONDAY, Nov. 7, 1864.

Took the 7 o'clock a. m. stage for Montpelier, and thence by 11 o'clock a. m. train to Vergennes to see Levi Meader, my old roommate at Barre Academy, Mr. F. E. Woodbridge's law partner; am not impressed with the cordiality of Mr. Woodbridge; met him on the train en route.

TUESDAY, Nov. 8, 1864.

It has rained all day. Well, this is a great day in the States! Probably more depends on what it brings forth than any since Washington's time. As for myself, though, I have no fear but what all will come out right; am still in Vergennes, and have voted for Abraham Lincoln—my first vote. The city's vote is as follows:

Lincoln   310

McClellan 15

Good! This is as it should be.

WEDNESDAY, Nov. 9, 1864.

Was shown the city by Meader today. Hon. F. E. Woodbridge, who is a representative in Congress, returned home from Washington last night. He is Meader's law partner; was introduced this morning; took the train for Williston, Vt. at 11 o'clock a. m. but being express didn't stop; arrived in Montpelier at 4 o'clock p. m.; shall stay here tonight; went to the theatre this evening.

THURSDAY, Nov. 10, 1864.

A gloomy, lonely day; visited the State House this afternoon; if in condition would like to return to the front; am at Burnham's Hotel; have been to the theatre; fine evening.

FRIDAY, Nov. 11, 1864.

Fair day; arrived in Barre by 7 o'clock p. m. stage; took my first degree in masonry to-night. Webber Tilden did the work.

SATURDAY, Nov. 12, 1864.

A cold bleak day; went up to James Burnham's with Fanny West this forenoon; took her and Cousin Pert and called on the Calefs and Alma Watson at Washington; returned to and stayed at James'; Ryle Seaver was there; had company in the evening.

SUNDAY, Nov. 13, 1864.

Snowed this morning; there's about three inches of snow on the ground tonight; left James Burnham's at 9 o'clock a. m. in a snowstorm; arrived at Barre just in season for William Old's funeral; have attended the funeral this afternoon at the Universalist Church of Lester Tilden. Captain Albert Dodge called this afternoon; has stopped snowing.

MONDAY, Nov. 14, 1864.

The Academy examinations commenced today; attended morning prayers. Mr. J. S. Spaulding looks and is the same as ever; nice old gentleman; called at the Curriers this evening; were glad to see me; clever old people; attended the examination of a class of youngsters in geography at the Academy.

TUESDAY, Nov. 15, 1864.

Attended the examination at the Academy of classes in mathematics to include geometry; nothing very exciting going on.

WEDNESDAY, Nov. 16, 1864.

Have passed a pleasant day; met James Abbott of Williamstown, Vt., this afternoon at the Academy; fine looking and a fine fellow, too; closing exercises come off at the Academy this evening. Carl Wilson and Frank French called tonight.

THURSDAY, Nov. 17, 1864.

Am in Montpelier tonight. Mr. and Mrs. David Mower and Cousin Pert are here, too; have been to the dentist's to have an impression taken for my new teeth; am to have them in the morning; went to the theatre tonight with George and Mrs. Watson; saw the good play of East Lynne; shall stay with them tonight; very cold and much snow; am getting worn-out with so much visiting.

FRIDAY, Nov. 18, 1864.

Have had some photographs taken; went up to the State House this forenoon, and afternoon; had a torchlight parade this evening; village illuminated; speeches by Governors Holbrook, Dillingham, etc. General Stannard present; didn't get my teeth.

SATURDAY, Nov. 19, 1864.

Cold with chilly north wind; stayed at Burnham's Hotel last night; hotel overcrowded; had to room with Mr. Orcutt of Roxbury; Captain Albert Dodge and wife and Louise Dodge in town; went to the depot with Mr. Orcutt; expect a visit from him in camp this winter; went up to the hospital with some ladies; arrived in Barre at 7 o'clock p. m.; took two degrees in masonry; am a Master Mason.

SUNDAY, Nov. 20, 1864.

Went to church this forenoon. Lester Hanson read a sermon, Mr. Bliss being in Woodstock, Vt.; went to Henry Burnham's funeral, a victim of the Civil War, in the afternoon at Williamstown; am at Uncle Howe's tonight; have called on Aunt Sarah Simons; weather threatening.

MONDAY, Nov. 21, 1864.

Not very cold; about two inches of snow on the ground this morning; went with Cousin Pert to Cousin David Smith's this forenoon, and then to Barre, arriving at Mr. David Mower's at 4 o'clock p. m.; raining hard to-night; have been to a Masonic meeting; saw Mr. Jones initiated.

TUESDAY, Nov. 22, 1864.

Northwest wind, cold and cloudy, with snow to-night; went up to the old homestead this afternoon; called at Mr. Elijah Wheeler's, also at his sister Susan's; am at Jim Burnham's to-night with Ryle Seaver; shall both stay here. Aunt Thompson has gone over to Cousin David Smith's.

WEDNESDAY, Nov. 23, 1864.

Pleasant and not very cold; started for Cousin David's at 9 o'clock a. m.; called at Mr. Flint's, at Rodney Seaver's and on Cousin Aurora Benedict; found Cousin Abby Howe at Ro's, too; took Thanksgiving dinner with Cousin Lois and David Smith's family, and went to Barre. Hattie Burnham is ill with diphtheria.

THURSDAY, Nov. 24, 1864.

Started for the front this morning at 6 o'clock, or rather for Annapolis, Md. Cousin Pert went as far as Bellows Falls with me; arrived at Springfield, Mass. at 8 o'clock, p. m., at N. Y. City about midnight, and daylight found me between Philadelphia and Baltimore.

FRIDAY, Nov. 25, 1864.

Arrived at Baltimore about 9 o'clock a. m.; remained at the Eutaw House until 4.40 o'clock p. m.; arrived at Annapolis at about 8 o'clock p. m.; reported to the surgeon in charge at once who ordered me to report to the Board of Examiners tomorrow morning; am in a room with two other officers.

SATURDAY, Nov. 26, 1864.

Reported at the Examiners' room at 9.30 o'clock a. m.; was ordered to report at 9.30 o'clock a. m. Monday; have been up town today; very dilapidated looking place and dull; hardly know what to do with myself. Three more officers have been assigned to my room tonight. There are quite a number of officers here from my Division.

SUNDAY, Nov. 27, 1864.

Warm and pleasant; nothing doing; have been lounging about and resting up; saw guard mounting this morning at the Marine Barracks and also at the post; hope I shan't have to remain here long, it's so dull; shall go to the front in the morning if they will let me.

MONDAY, Nov. 28, 1864.

Well, this has been an interesting day, a great surprise; have been treated with great consideration—like a prince—by the board, and I never saw one of them before, nor had they ever heard of me that I know of. They made my mouth wound of so much interest it embarrassed me; I felt as though I was being lionized. The board is composed of a General and several other elderly medical officers of rank and age, and they have the consideration and tact—unlike Dr. Thayer—to treat any wounded officer and especially one who fought with Sheridan at Winchester, with distinguished respect. The first one who looked at my wound expressed great surprise at my "unusually interesting mouth wound," as he termed it, and called for the doctors in the adjoining rooms to come and see one of the most interesting of the many wounds that had come before the board. They all came, each in turn examining it, expressing great wonder, and asked many questions, indignantly inquiring why the Vermont doctors had sent me back to the front with jaws in a condition such as to render it impossible for me to chew solid food when it was known that hard bread and meats were the principal articles of food for troops in the field and with the stitches still in my lip and it not solidly healed. In reply I gave them my experience with Dr. Thayer of Burlington, Vt., and said I had not gone to the hospital several times during the war because of my pride and fear of inconsiderate treatment, although I had ought to have gone twice before when wounded, but feared I might be criticised if I did. They continued to examine the wound for some time expressing astonishment that it should have healed as much as it had so soon and would leave so little trace or scar externally in the end as it would, and highly complimented Dr. Rutherford who attended me. They finally drew aside for consultation, and when the examiner who had charge of the case returned and said that I could have my choice, take my discharge or return to the front, I was delighted, and chose the latter. He seemed surprised, and after hesitating a little looking steadily at me, said I had better consider the matter well; but I told him I had, that I could soak my hard bread in water, fry it with salt pork which would make it both soft and nutritious, and that I could get along. Seeing that I really wanted to return, he let me go. I received my discharge from the hospital this afternoon, have got my transportation, and shall leave to-morrow at 2 o'clock p. m. Captain Mattison, a fine little fellow, left this afternoon. We are all in good spirits to-night. But the Annapolis board of surgeons were clever gentlemen. Their sympathy and consideration was unusual.

TUESDAY, Nov. 29, 1864.

Left Annapolis for Baltimore on the 1 o'clock p. m. train; waited at Annapolis Junction an hour and arrived in Baltimore about dark; am at the Eutaw House to-night; no one here I know; very dull; shall start for the front to-morrow.

WEDNESDAY, Nov. 30, 1864.

Took the 9 o'clock a. m. train for the west; lots of passengers going to the front; found a freight train off the track at Ellicott Mills, Md.; was about two hours late at Harper's Ferry where I stop over night; shall take the first train to the front in the morning; no news; very dull here.

Thursday, Dec. 1, 1864.

Well, I am a nine months' man! Good (?) I went into General Stevenson's headquarters and found the Tenth Vermont was at Petersburg. He ordered me to report to Col. Hunter commanding Camp Distribution at Harper's Ferry; was ordered to take command of the Twentieth Company, Sixth Corps—about 200 men; have got to receipt for clothing, camp equipage, etc.; don't like it, but have to obey orders. The camp is on a barren, bleak side hill long used for such a purpose, and it is cold, windy and dirty with a great deal of dust. I don't like the prospect.

Friday, Dec. 2, 1864.

Cold and windy; no quarters or accommodations of any kind; have been down to General Stevenson's to get relieved, but he won't listen to it; went later to Colonel Hunter to get permission to go down town to sleep, but he won't let me go; am to stay with the Quartermaster to-night; have drawn fifty-four shelter tents for the men who are out of everything are blue at having to stay here, and everything's depressing. I am glad they are good men; wish I was out of this.

Saturday, Dec. 3, 1864.

Cold as ever; got an old rotten, dirty wall tent and put it up; took the men's receipts for shelter tents; fingers very cold and numb from writing; camp dirty; men complaining because they have no clothes; quartermaster ordered to his regiment; no one to issue clothing. Oh, dear! When will I get out of this? I'm disgusted with the management here. General Stevenson wants to put me on his staff as Depot Quartermaster at Harper's Ferry; sent for me and urged me to accept; told him I preferred a fighting position to the end of the war with my regiment at the front; think he was vexed with me, but I can't help it. I'm no shirk from battle if I have been four times wounded! I'm no quitter! besides I don't want to be filled with remorse in years to come that I shirked the front when needed. I propose to be able to look any man in the eye without flinching on that score.

Sunday, Dec. 4, 1864.

Weather more comfortable this morning; more convalescents, etc., reporting in small squads; am feeling some better, but *do* want to go to my regiment: men complaining, but I can't help it, there's no quartermaster; am busy with clothing rolls; looks like storm to-night.

Monday, Dec. 5, 1864.

Cold northeast wind; am told by the Commanding Officer I shall probably get an order to go to Washington to-night; am hurrying to finish my clothing rolls; twenty men reported to-night for the Ninth N. Y. Infantry; don't believe I shall get an order to move after all to-night. Well I suppose this is all necessary to make a soldier!

Tuesday, Dec. 6, 1864.

Laid out Company streets and had the men police; got a man to build me a chimney; don't smoke; am feeling better; men in better spirits, but anxious to go to their regiments; have had forty men turned over to my command without tents, overcoats or blankets; had an interesting, good man report belonging to the Fourth N. J. Infantry, who can help me, and I like him; don't like being commanding officer and everything else, though; too much to do to look after a regiment of men without even a clerk. But they are good, and seem to like to be with me, for they are all the time wanting to do something for me—probably because I try to make them comfortable.

Wednesday, Dec. 7, 1864.

Pleasant and warm in the morning, but the wind began to blow about noon, and to-night it's quite uncomfortable. My clerk has quite an interesting history, and I like him the more I see of him; got an order about 3 o'clock p. m. to get my men in readiness for the cars for Washington; left about 9 o'clock p. m. in a rainstorm.

Thursday, Dec. 8, 1864.

Arrived at Washington Junction at daylight; were delayed by freight trains till 8 o'clock a. m.; arrived in Washington about 10 o'clock a. m. A man got shot in the foot; got breakfast at the Soldiers Rest; am in charge of the guard. Colonel Hunter and the Adjutant are up town looking for General Wright; am to stay in town to-night.

Friday, Dec. 9, 1864.

Stopped at the National Hotel last night; looks like snow this morning; got my pay this forenoon; returned to the Soldiers Rest about noon; men in good spirits. Colonel Hunter was relieved this morning by Major Jones; men started for the front this afternoon at 4 o'clock; hated to lose them. I leave on the government boat to-morrow for City Point.

Saturday, Dec. 10, 1864.

Stayed at the Kirkwood last night; roomed with Captain Briggs of the One Hundred and Sixth N. Y. Infantry, but he was out all night; went to the German Opera at Grover's Theater last evening; about four inches of snow on the ground this morning; sailed with Captain Briggs for City Point at 3 o'clock p. m.; dull, and cold wind down the river.

SUNDAY, Dec. 11, 1864.

Arrived at Fortress Monroe at 7 o'clock a. m.; grand old place; never saw so much shipping at one time before; left for City Point at 9 o'clock a. m. arriving about 3 o'clock p. m.; stayed with Lieut. S. H. Lewis, Jr. till 5 o'clock p. m.; arrived at brigade headquarters about 8 o'clock p. m.; shall stay with Lieut. H. W. Kingsley to-night.

MONDAY, Dec. 12, 1864.

Very cold all day; remained with Kingsley until about 11 o'clock a. m. and then went over to the regiment some distance away; found the men stationed at Ft. Dushane doing garrison duty. Colonel W. W. Henry has sent in his resignation; sorry to lose him; has been the most popular field officer we have ever had, all and all. Major L. T. Hunt has gone for good. Colonel C. G. Chandler has been courtmartialed; will probably go home; shall stay with Dr. Almon Clark; quarters in a house near the fort; men are without quarters; have never seen the regiment so uncomfortably fixed.

TUESDAY, Dec. 13, 1864.

Not quite so cold. Captain A. W. Chilton and Lieut. Wheeler came off picket this morning; no orders to put up quarters; wonder if some of the officers are not getting faint-hearted and getting out of it; no one can accuse me of it after declining my discharge at Annapolis and General Stevenson's offer. I find the army in poor spirits; needs rest, at any rate Sheridan's Shenandoah Valley part of it; give it rest and it will be all right for another campaign. These enormous earthworks in our front seem to give everybody the nightmare, but I anticipate a weakly manned part of the line will be found, easily broken, and then, as the enemy is disheartened, goodbye, Johnny! The next campaign will be virtually the last.

WEDNESDAY, Dec. 14, 1864.

Has been quite warm and comfortable all day; dull in camp, and no news from Generals Sherman or Thomas; got an order to fix up quarters this morning which will do the men good as it will occupy their minds; are getting out timber now; shall be glad when my hut is fixed; am tired of changing about so much; wrote to Jim Burnham this evening; expected to go on duty this morning.

THURSDAY, Dec. 15, 1864.

Very warm and comfortable all day; am on duty in the fort; have a guard of one Sergeant, three Corporals and thirty-six men; duty easy; rumors from General Thomas this evening but nothing reliable; got a letter from Cousin Pert to-day; no news from Oakdale, Mass.; was very sorry to learn of G. B. Putnam's death.

FRIDAY, Dec. 16, 1864.

Warm and pleasant; trains busy drawing hut timber; was relieved from guard by the One Hundred and Thirty-eighth Pennsylvania Infantry; am not feeling well; received a letter from David Mower and have answered it; all well in Vermont; Captain H. H. Dewey and Lieutenant Daniel Foster, Tenth Vermont, reported for duty this morning from City Point; have been ill in hospital there; had an undress parade this evening; good news from Thomas. Lieutenant Alexander Wilkey starts for home in the morning.

SATURDAY, Dec. 17, 1864.

Fair, comfortable day; men busy putting up quarters; shall commence my hut when the men finish theirs; good news from Generals Sherman and Thomas this evening; have written Dr. J. H. Jones this evening; southeast storm brewing; cannonading towards Petersburg to-night; nothing unusual.

SUNDAY, Dec. 18, 1864.

Quite comfortable all day. Colonel W. W. Henry's resignation came back last night accepted; will leave at 7.40 o'clock a. m. to-morrow; officers gave him a farewell supper to-night. Captain G. B. Damon comes back to the regiment to-night from the division staff. I have been recommended for the Captaincy of Company G overslaughing several other officers, provided he is made Major; all's quiet.

MONDAY, Dec. 19, 1864.

Colonel W. W. Henry started for Vermont this morning; most of the officers of the regiment went to the cars to see him off; commenced raining about 8 o'clock a. m.; didn't rain long; men very busy on their cabins; got a Washington Chronicle to-night; good news from Generals Sherman and Thomas, the latter having captured fifty eight guns and five thousand prisoners.

TUESDAY, Dec. 20, 1864.

It's rumored we are to move camp in a day or two; wish they would allow us to stay here; had monthly inspection at 3 o'clock p. m.; men in good condition considering. Captain Day was our inspecting officer. Captain G. E. Davis has gone to City Point; returned at 9 o'clock p. m.; got me two wool blankets; rumored in camp Jeff Davis is dead; don't believe it.

WEDNESDAY, Dec. 21, 1864.

Rained hard most of the day from 7 o'clock a. m.; have suspended work on the huts; expect to move in a few days; very muddy in camp; clear, cold north wind and freezing at 9 o'clock p. m.; news still good from Sherman and Thomas.

THURSDAY, Dec. 22, 1864.

Cold and windy; froze about four inches last night. Captain Bartruff has been over to call on us; says that we will have to move over with the rest of the brigade to-morrow, but why were we told to build quarters here? Pretty rough, but we shall have to stand it! Glorious news from General Thomas to-night; has captured sixty-one pieces of artillery and nine thousand prisoners. We move at 9 o'clock a. m. to-morrow.

FRIDAY, Dec. 23, 1864.

Moved at 8 o'clock a. m.; weather freezing cold; only seven teams at work with us; regiment excused from brigade dress parade this evening. It's *very* cold to-night; shall sleep on Captain G. E. Davis's floor; men are without quarters; should think they would freeze. It's rumored Savannah is captured; doubt it.

SATURDAY, Dec. 24, 1864.

Very cold, but more comfortable than yesterday; commenced putting up my cabin this morning; not quite up to-night; regimental dress parade this evening. General Butler's fleet is off Wilmington; Savannah, Ga. reported captured through rebel sources; have written to David Mower, and to Washington for my valise; weather moderating; all's quiet in front.

SUNDAY, Dec. 25, 1864.

Rained all night; very muddy; working hard to finish my house by to-morrow night; had 10.30 o'clock a. m. Company inspection; various rumors about General Sherman; news good from General Thomas; good regimental dress parade this evening.

MONDAY, Dec. 26, 1864.

Received official information from General Sherman this morning that he had taken Savannah, Ga. with thirty-three thousand bales of cotton, one hundred and fifty heavy guns, and eight hundred prisoners; one hundred shotted guns fired in honor of it here; Thomas reports seventeen thousand prisoners, eighty-one guns, etc., taken from General Hood; no news from the Shenandoah Valley; rumored in camp that the Eighth Corps is at Dutch Gap; hut covered and banked up; regimental dress parade to-night; mud drying up; reckon the Confederacy is crumbling rapidly.

TUESDAY, Dec. 27, 1864.

Quite decent under foot; hut about done; shall move into it to-morrow night. Captain Merritt Barber has been over and turned over Company E property to me; good brigade dress parade this evening; had a call from Lieut. Pierce of the Second Division to-night; have written Levi Meader this evening; am to be brigade officer of the guard to-morrow.

WEDNESDAY, Dec. 28, 1864.

Mounted brigade guard at 8.30 o'clock a. m. as officer of the guard; northeast chilly wind; brigade dress parade this evening; Tenth Vermont worked on breastworks this forenoon; finished my cabin to-day; wrote brother Charles this evening; received a letter and diary for 1865 from Cousin Pert; weather very rough to-night.

THURSDAY, Dec. 29, 1864.

Weather has moderated since morning; quite muddy; had two hours battalion drill; think it a big thing on ice. In my opinion we would look better in the house, and I am sure we should feel better; got a letter from Dr. J. H. Jones to-night. He was married Nov. 8, 1864; received our muster and pay rolls to-day; have commenced a part of two; hard cold north wind to-night. Sergeant Charles of the One Hundred and Fifty-first New York is here to-night.

FRIDAY, Dec. 30, 1864.

Worked all day on muster and pay rolls; mild south wind; storm brewing. Captain G. E. Davis drilled the battalion this afternoon in the manual of arms; muddy brigade dress parade this evening; hardly a gun to be heard on picket to-night; no letters or news; retired at 11 o'clock p. m. tired.

SATURDAY, Dec. 31, 1864.

Well, here I am again in winter quarters, but how different from twelve months ago. I confess, though, that my prayer has been answered, the year having been passed as happily by me as could have been expected under the circumstances. I have been called upon to pass through a great many ordeals but with God's grace have come out alive. I shudder when I think how many have been killed out of our little band, yet I am spared perhaps for some good purpose; I hope so, anyway. I'm about to commence another year. I feel sad to bid the old one farewell. It has been a strenuous, eventful and historic one.

May the next end the war, if it is God's will.